THE REVOLUTION OF 2012

Volume One: The Preparation

Andrew Smith

FORD-EVANS PUBLISHING

The Revolution of 2012
Vol 1 The Preparation

First published 2006
ISBN 0 9512961 4 0

A catalogue entry for this book is available from The British Library

Cover Pastel by Christine Evans
Cover Design and Layout by Jessie Ford
Published in the UK by Ford-Evans Publishing

Distribution Enquiries to:

distribution@revolutionof2012.net

or mail to

Pengerd Cottage, West Pennard, Glastonbury, Somerset, BA6 8NH

Printed in England by Wincanton Print Company Ltd

CONTENTS

ACKNOWLEDGMENT AND DEDICATION

I would like to acknowledge the inspiration and loving support from the Spiritual Realms in the creation of this book and the following volumes. Firstly, I am very thankful to the Hermetic, the Old Chinese, and the Etruscan healer for the first stage of my Spiritual education. In more recent years, I am deeply grateful to Archangel Metatron, Archangel Michael, Mother Meera, Masters El Morya, Kuthumi, Serapis Bey, Kuan Yin, St. Germain and the Etruscan for their loving inspiration, illumination, encouragement, and patient explanations. I further thank and dedicate this work to the beauty, warmth, and creativity of the Divine Feminine as she reintegrates into the new essence of evolving Humanity.

My heartfelt thanks to my wife Patricia for the hours spent on word processing and her unlimited love and support. Loving thanks to my son Leon for setting up and managing the book website. I am very grateful to my brother David for helping to fund the printing of this book. Special appreciation to Ann Evans, Jessie Ford and Christine Evans of Ford-Evans Publishing for the cover design and advice on creative marketing. Many thanks also to John McClaughlin, Grethe Hooper Hansen, and Philip O'Donohoe for their meticulous reviews of the manuscript and insightful suggestions.

PROLOGUE

The wheat field spread before me rolling gently downhill as I approached the Crop Circle. The farmer's tractor wheels had left twin corridors through the wheat crop, which had already grown some three feet in height. I could see in the near distance other curving corridors moving off on either side and some circular images beyond.

I took the first curving corridor and followed it round until it opened out into a large circle. With geometric precision, some invisible hand had divided the stalks growing vertically from those lying horizontally on the ground, creating a circular wall of wheat. The horizontal stalks swirled around the circle as if a mini tornado of incredible precision had touched down.

I was drawn to a point on the edge of the swirling circle – my hands tingled with incoming energy and I was moved to lie down on the carpet of wheat. I closed my eyes and a great wave of relief and joy flowed through my whole being. My physical body was in total peace and harmony, a feeling of timelessness permeated my mind, my emotional body transmuted to an ocean of harmonious feeling, of a heightened sense of being and unity with all spheres, of unlimitedness beyond any constraint. A voice inside my head said, "Welcome to Fifth Dimensional Consciousness".

PART ONE:

THE CHANGING WORLD

CHAPTER ONE
The Initial Approach

During a morning meditation in March 2002, I was approached by a Spiritual Presence with a strongly feminine essence who communicated that an account needed to be written down and published describing the enormous evolutionary changes facing the Earth during the ensuing decade and beyond.

They shared that, during the years going forward to the Winter Solstice of 2012, the Earth would be changing and evolving on a scale beyond precedent. It was time for the Earth to rejoin the other planets in the Solar System, which long ago evolved to Fifth Dimensional Consciousness and even beyond. The Earth has stayed at a third dimensional consciousness level for untold thousands of years, held back from natural progression by an "arm lock" of global proportions, installed and sustained by Astral entities, originating particularly from the darkness pertaining to the end of the Atlantean age. The Earth needed to evolve to Fifth Dimensional consciousness both for her own evolution and for the needs of the whole Solar System to itself grow and evolve. Humans were invited to undertake this great journey also, provided they were willing to go through the required process of Attunement to the new Spiritual Design.

Restoration of the Divine Order

She revealed that an important key to this Spiritual Design was going to be the re-establishment of the Divine Feminine in full balance and harmony with the Divine Masculine. This would be part of a comprehensive restoration of the Divine Order, which had been the foundation of life on Earth prior to Humanity's "Fall from Grace" during the latter phase of the Atlantean civilisation. The days of a one-sided predominantly masculine era were numbered.

I realised that these changes seemed to interface naturally with the implicit prophecy built into the old Mayan calendars, which reach back at least three thousand years. According to Carlos Barrios in his book "Kam Wuj, El Libro del Destino", the Fourth World, of a highly materialistic nature, finished on 16th August, 1987, the day of the Harmonic Convergence. At that time the World entered a time of major transition, during which there will be a colossal, global, convergence of environmental destruction, social chaos, war, and on-going Earth changes. This in-between period will continue until the Winter Solstice 2012. It will be a time of rebirth, the beginning of the Fifth World, a new era when peace begins and people live in harmony with Mother Earth, a time of fusion and integration of Life and Light. The Spiritual Presence went on to describe how this overall account would set out the Creation of a New World vibrating at more refined wavelengths, strongly based on the Love and Light naturally emanating from an open and attuned Heart, with the mental and physical faculties in a balanced service role.

This fundamental shift would change our lives on Earth in every field of endeavour. The current foundation belief of contemporary mankind that the Earth exists primarily for the human race, and its continued existence, will be replaced by the balanced perspective that Humanity is a valued participant in life on Earth, when appropriately attuned to Spirit and fully respectful of all living kingdoms and their inhabitants. Just as the old belief that the Sun rotated around the Earth was replaced with the truth that the Earth was the one doing the orbiting, so humans need to understand that the profound evolutionary needs of the Earth are paramount.

Although extensive preparations are envisaged, or are already underway, to address the needs of the human population throughout the coming extraordinary course of change, all such plans are subordinate to the primary direction and grand scale of transition by the Earth and the Solar System as a whole. The choice for Humanity is the extent to which each person wishes to release the old patterns of living and adapt to the dynamic realities of the Earth's transition – rather like running down the platform to board a moving train. And this would need to be repeated at a variety of different "stations" as new phases of evolution commenced, requiring further shedding of old ways and old places, and the embracing of yet another new dynamic.

After a few weeks reflection and some Spiritual encouragement, I began writing down this somewhat extraordinary narration. It has been a voyage of great discovery as paragraph after paragraph revealed itself. It must be emphasised that this is a channelled book – I personally had at best a modest knowledge of the main themes presented and, in particular, how they interrelated with each other. My own life changed dramatically as I moved from Marin County, California to rural England, after living in the United States for some twenty three years. I embrace the Illumined Path forward.

Working with "The Revolution of 2012"

"The Preparation" is the first volume of three comprising "The Revolution of 2012". It presents a description of the profound changes in the Cosmic Energy Environment on Earth during the years preceding 2012. The purpose of the book is to provide a coherent description and explanation of dramatic changes to the Earth, and those of us who dwell upon Her, during the years preceding 2012.

In this volume, we start by describing the evolutionary plans of the Earth for the next decade or so. We go on to examine the implications for mankind and the other species who call Earth their home. The very many assumptions which make up what we perceive as the foundations of "life on Earth" are changing in a major way, and an appreciable number are changing out of all recognition. Some of these assumptions are less well known than others, but their importance and contribution exist, irrespective of the visibility of their profile.

There are specific sections on the overall vision within the Spiritual Design as it manifests in each aspect of life, reflecting the essence and effect of the re-emerging Divine Feminine in establishing balance and harmony with the Divine Masculine. Subsequent chapters will go into detail as to how this may impact all areas of life involvement. We shall address how individuals can attune to a deeper reality even while the structures around them are in flux.

The last part of the book addresses the extraordinary nature of the culmination of the Spiritual Design in 2012 and how we can best address the personal challenge of our individual evolution throughout the process.

THE INITIAL APPROACH

The reader is invited to Attune with the new energies and implement and/or align with them to the greatest possible extent in all parts of life during this time of transition. The second part of this volume describes application of these principles to the main arenas of life. It is recommended that the reader enters into a process of exploration and experimentation of their own to see how these new approaches to life can evolve in the most positive way.

Although the Fifth-Dimensional post-2012 world is projected to be radically different from the current era, it is suggested that the reader will be much better prepared to address that changed world if they have done the work of opening their Heart Centre and experienced the great deepening and balancing of their interface with all aspects of Life. They will be well positioned to understand and address "The Challenge" of choosing an evolutionary Path set out in volume two of "The Revolution of 2012". This leads in turn to "Taking Action" described in volume three.

Throughout this writing, it will be noticed that various phrases describing new Sacred terms begin with capital letters like "Fifth Dimensional Consciousness" and "Cosmic Illumination". This is used to represent Spirit and the Godforce penetrating deeply into every part of the Earth and our world upon Her.

CHAPTER TWO
An Outline of the Spiritual Design

The Earth's transition is happening, come what may. The paramount choice for humanity is the extent to which we individually change and adapt to the new realities each remaining year, including the need for re-integration of the Divine Feminine in all aspects of society.

Each of us depends critically on the flow of Spiritual Light through our beings for the very sustenance of life in our physical bodies. As the wavelengths of this Spiritual Light become more and more refined, there is less and less life support for individuals in traditional third dimensional modes of living. This seemingly harsh reality lends considerable urgency to the need to attune at a Heart level to the evolutionary requirements of this Spiritual Design, during the transition period through the Winter Solstice 2012. After this point, there will not be any Spiritual life-support for individuals without Fifth Dimensional Consciousness. Staying on the Earth will no longer be a viable option for them. Their evolutionary path will naturally take them to new lives on other planets in the Galaxy, still at third or fourth dimensional levels, where they will find a new home which matches their current vibrational and evolutionary needs.

This is truly a wake-up call so that all of us, who love the Earth and wish to stay onboard, can complete the necessary inner work of Attunement with Fifth Dimensional consciousness and the release of prior karmic patterns. The good news is that there is, and will continue to be, much support available for individuals learning to function at these higher levels of consciousness. The opening of the Heart Centre together with a strong inner commitment will be an essential step for individuals to attune with and tangibly live these higher vibrational realities. The explicit re-admittance of the Divine Feminine to a full participation in all Humanity's activities and realities will be a critical element in the softening of all aspects of Earthly life.

Alignment with the New Path

This account is devoted to a revelation of how the implementation of this major Spiritual Design is changing fundamentally the experience of being an individual human being, as well as changing the societal and nation-states' structures, which surround us. We are in a time of radical change, indeed the most profound revolution in our recorded history. The scale of the changes is such that many myths will be recounted about them in future ages. One purpose of these writings is to help the reader prepare themselves to thrive in the midst of turmoil and, as Rudyard Kipling once put it, "to keep your head while those all around you are losing theirs".

Our intent is to provide a coherent description of the Path of evolutionary change which the Earth is taking so that the reader has the opportunity to consciously choose to understand and align themselves harmoniously with that path. If one knows the broad outline and general direction of the changes, one can more readily place the unfolding events in a meaningful context. Preparations can be made for riding the evolutionary wave instead of being submerged by it. Plans can be altered thoughtfully in measured response to various manifestations of Nature's events.

Some parts of the world are more in tune with the new direction of change than others. There are groups within societies where loving friendship, compassionate caring, a generosity of sharing, male/female balance, and service to others are normal facets of everyday living. They will come through the next years in much better condition than other groups based on the development and expression of ego and its associated traits of self-aggrandisement.

As the vibrational frequency of the Earth continually rises month by month, the values, actions, and ways of living which created some degree of worldly outward success for the last century or so, will no longer deliver the same kind of outcomes. This may not be immediately obvious for it is in the nature of mankind to adopt some formula for living which has worked reasonably well in one time period and then to enshrine this particular approach to life in a self-sustaining cloak of irreproachability. Once so enshrined, it is believed that little can be changed, even when all external circumstances and inner intuition cry out for a new direction. Indeed many religions, philosophies, and political movements bear witness to these various states of suspended animation.

So, in this period of radical and dramatic evolution during the run-up to 2012, reactions at all levels of society will instinctively seek to place unique, unfolding events within some existing paradigm of understanding and explanation. Instead, there is a great need to recognise new departures from the status quo as the genuinely new events and changes which are really happening.

Governments particularly will seek to re-assure their citizenry that "nothing really has changed" when a disastrous flood, a major earthquake, treble strength hurricanes, or new volcanoes erupting cause widespread devastation. "Are these not merely random disasters which Nature inflicts upon Humanity every 100 years or so?" These hazardous events, it will be maintained publicly, are just part of the normal risks for Humans living on Earth. Instead of acting as a higher source of knowledge, governments will tend to obscure the gravity of the changing situation through defensive and self-justifying responses, and lull many of their citizens back to complacency and inner sleep.

Although some environmentally conscious individuals may relate the "natural disasters" to imbalances caused by destruction of the rain forests, other misuses of the land, pollution of the air, rivers, and seas, as well as contamination underground, they would tend to see the dramatic events taking place primarily as a logical consequence of the environmental causes alone, rather than the initial stages of a fundamental transition by the Earth. We experience these rearrangements of the Earth's physical being merely from our location on the surface. It will greatly help our understanding of the evolving Spiritual Design if we can relate to the Earth's experience and needs more holistically.

CHAPTER THREE
A Vision of a New World

In this chapter we share a vision of life on Earth, for those who may choose the ascent to Fifth Dimensional Consciousness over the next six years or so. It is a vision which encompasses every life-form and every activity upon the Earth and reflects the profound transformation taking place in each one of us. As the underlying vibrational pattern mutates to higher and higher octaves, we adopt the resonance of fundamentally new scales.

An attempt to describe Fifth Dimensional Consciousness at this stage can provide little more than some entry points into a much greater journey of exploration. It is certainly not necessary to enter a crop circle to experience this level of Consciousness, even though that is a very direct way to access it, should it be available. So let's set out an outline of the new patterns in order to perceive their manifestation within all the arenas of life we can experience while incarnated within human physical form. We can keep these patterns in mind as we visit each arena.

Words are not adequate or sufficient to describe this level of consciousness, which is essentially non-verbal. But in the Spirit of Illuminating Truth, the following concepts may relate:

A continuous awareness of connection to all that is.

An eternal sense of belonging.

A growing perception of how our part of the evolving Divine Plan relates to a greater whole.

Communication by multidimensional waves of meaning, feeling, understanding, and Illumination.

Unlimited creative endeavour.

Abundance of resources allied to a wisdom regarding their balanced use.

Connection with Spirit and Universal Presence

A continual loving connection with Spirit is the foundation of the new paradigms of life on Earth as she evolves to Fifth Dimensional consciousness. Going beyond the regular occasions of connection through meditation, prayer, and the other special times of inward reflection, we can move into a state of continual awareness of the Universal Presence, at both a cellular and a Heart level.

This profound change of orientation will come about quite naturally as the Light vibrational patterns become more readily available, not only through lying on the floor of a crop circle, finding an enchanted place beside a woodland stream or maybe a special place within a meditation garden, but as we go about our daily tasks and daily interactions with our fellow human beings, this identity with Spirit will be all pervading. It will show itself through the expression of Heart-felt warmth, joy, and compassion integrated into each communication and action within an ongoing flow.

Over the last millennium, the ideas and conceptualisation of an ideal world, a utopian dream, even a Heaven on Earth, have provided the subject matter for many learned treatises, as well as inspired paintings depicting such idyllic existences. Often the underlying themes are driven by a wish to eliminate all the difficulties or harsh features of the writer's or artist's contemporary world. What is left is at least benign and often associated with a desirable lifestyle of leisure, sunshine, inspiration, freedom and bonhomie, within a traditional primary orientation of materialism.

It is proposed that a quite different and more rewarding approach is to look at every aspect of life and imagine or perceive excellent ongoing situations coming into being in which individuals can and do thrive amidst universal values and conditions of: "Alignment with the One", plenty, good health, peacefulness and harmony, widespread creativity and universal love. The immediate and inevitable questions come up around each of these groups of universal values and conditions– "what does each of them really comprise? What is actually meant by these fine sounding epithets and what are the subtle, less obvious components of these feelings of universal excellence? What kinds of consciousness enable us to visualise and feel all these facets of an Illuminated state of being?

Spiritual teachers throughout the ages have consistently pointed the way towards the understanding that Spiritual Growth transpires as an individual re-directs their attention and focus from the outside world to go within, to an inner world. In that place and state, all things become possible, miracles are a further extension of sustained manifestation, imagination and delight are like in-breaths and out-breaths. Creation becomes a mainstream state of consciousness, while original and "in the now" manifestation replaces the repetitious nature of "what has been" being continually reproduced by an individual's sub-conscious mind.

Cosmic Illumination

One of the least understood influences on both the course of world events and the state of individual consciousness is that of Cosmic Illumination. These patterns of focussed intervention by the Spiritual Hierarchy stimulate the awakening of consciousness in specific arenas of human existence and are at the root of major changes in life on Earth. This directed use of Spiritual Light to lift up inspirationally our Consciousness in the Now, allows individuals to glimpse and often absorb a higher experience of life in the physical world, side by side with their current "hands on" state of existence. This stimulation greatly enhances Spiritual Consciousness in general, as well as individual creativity. It enables the Spiritual World to influence the course of change of human evolution through creative endeavour.

For several thousand years these interventions have helped to prevent the Earth from disappearing into spiritual oblivion. Because of the dense state of the earthplane existence throughout this period, usually only one or two regions of the world were chosen at any one time for Cosmic Illumination. The concentration of effort produced tangible results for a while, Old China, Ancient Greece, Camelot, the Italian Renaissance, Britain in the early 1940s, San Francisco in the later 1960s, etc. But as the Spiritual intervention moved on, each of the chosen areas partially reverted back to the contemporary level of surrounding territories, while sometimes retaining key aspects of the Spiritual Intervention for an extended period.

Over the last two decades, the Spiritual Intervention to upgrade the earthplane consciousness has evolved to an unprecedented scale of intensity. No longer is the focus on one particular region being subject to Cosmic Illumination; rather these special energies are being applied world-wide.

In the last few years, the Spiritual Energy infusing the Earth has ratcheted up many notches, making a proverbial quantum leap in magnitude and breadth of application. The impact of this energy appears to vary considerably from location to location and from context to context. But they all have an underlying common process of inducing a release of negativity by laying down a carpet of high vibrational Light energy. As this carpet sinks deeper in to the land, it raises the vibration of all life that it touches and, in the process, forces the old, the stagnant and the burnt out residues to come to the surface. We have seen this pattern in the former Yugoslavia, in the Middle East, in Africa, as well as in other places. The actual behavioural content of these residues ranges through duplicity, betrayal, and persecution, or similar; laced with often horrific scenes of mass killing, torture, and other barbarities.

The prominence given to the news accounts of such bestial events makes it quite challenging to see the involvement of Light Energy at all, let alone the first beginnings of a major energy upgrade. Yet within the sayings of folklore, there are insights which directly support the more optimistic scenario of movement towards Light; “It’s always darkest before the dawn”,

"Every cloud has a silver lining", or more generally, "Things aren't what they seem to be".

Understanding the Transition

Questions which naturally arise around this overall transition from darkness to Light are: "How long does it take?", "Whereabouts in the process are we now?", and "How will we know when the changeover is finally completed?" Well, recognising the state of a shift in Light-Consciousness is rather like attempting to aggregate intangibles. However, the hundredth monkey syndrome is a useful analogy for this sense of reaching a critical mass of belief and behaviour patterns, which then becomes the new norm, and is observable as such.

Yet while the changes and shifts are underway, it is quite challenging trying to understand what is going on at any one point in time. The good news is that one doesn't have to know the specific details beyond an overall sense of the direction and content of the changes, with which we can choose to align ourselves. This may be coupled with a vision of that idyllic State of Being where Alignment with the One, plenty, good-health, peacefulness, creativity and universal love abound. In the interim an ongoing driving force of Inspiration provides the link between "what is now" and "what is coming".

Need for a Fundamental Approach in Depth

It is vital that we keep clearly in mind our vision of an unlimited New World, so that our thoughts, feelings, words and actions can be consistent with its creation, rather than taking the form of a day to day, week to week reaction to current situations. Although the latter often seem to cry out for our immediate attention to achieve at least a "quick fix", the new Spiritual energies now bathing the Earth require a more fundamental approach to finding solutions.

For example, in seeking to address the gruesome cycles of violence in Palestine and Israel, it is necessary to go right back to look at the energies pertaining in the late 1940s when the State of Israel was coalesced. What reign of terror caused hundreds of thousands of existing Palestinian inhabitants to leave their homes and flee for their lives or, in thousands of cases, be killed instead? How can this particular terror be condoned and institutionalised whilst subsequent acts of terror committed by the displaced population and their descendants are denounced? The truth about terror needs to be spoken of consistently, unmodified by political spin and expediency.

It is becoming more and more apparent that a stable, long term solution to sharing the land and resources for all the peoples of Palestine and Israel can only come about from a fundamentally honest recognition of what has happened at each stage, including all the events which do not suit the current myths and justifications. The former Truth and Reconciliation Commission in South Africa provided a useful example for defusing the deep memories and cycles of killing, terror and revenge.

On this foundation of truth, and recognition of each individual's right to live peacefully and productively, a new society of habitable villages and towns linked to sustainable water supplies, balanced agriculture and relevant light industry could be envisioned and constructed. The vast funds devoted to building and operating military organisations would go a long way to financing the constructions of the much needed new habitations and work environments.

The original kind of idealism which was present in the first decades of Israel needs to be brought back to life in the context of building a new pattern of groups of communities for all the inhabitants of the area, Palestinians as well as Israeli settlers. The Israeli talent for practical technological innovation needs to be applied consistently for the benefit of all communities and would be an important factor in creating a more sustainable prosperity and peaceful balance throughout the area. Overall, there would be a substantial energy upgrade towards the Light for everybody there.

A less dramatic but equally relevant example of uplifting change would be in the often troubled field of employer/employee relations, affecting most parts of the world. Many large corporations are untouched by the inspirational Light coming through Human Resources Development projects or Job Satisfaction teams. The employer faction, represented by the board of directors and senior management, is all too often in a state of continuous hostilities with the mass of employees, whether organised or not. The form of hostilities varies on the employer side from general low level harassment of staff by creating employment insecurity, to ongoing campaigns to demand more work for less remuneration. On the employee side, hardened attitudes and reactions postulate that no changes proposed by the employers can ever be of any benefit whatsoever to the workforce. Vast amounts of energy are consumed year after year in this frustrating standoff, without any real results beyond further aggravation and employee alienation.

In marked contrast, many small businesses work as a unified team. One of the boss's functions is to ensure that all his employees' needs are met in order that they can be fully productive, along with a strong sense of self-empowerment to achieve the daily needs of the business. The ongoing face to face relationship of employer and employee demands and enables an honesty of approach and personal interaction, as well as facilitating a similar level of business information.

Fortunately, some large organisations have "seen the Light" and realised that an operational regime based on self-empowerment of each employee will be to everyone's benefit. The availability and mobility of information at all levels will free up large amounts of time and energy for much improved creativity, inspiration, and productivity. Sustainable prosperity through open and consistent co-operation is the likely consequence of this more Enlightened approach to working life.

Stepping onto the Path of Light

It is this Vision of a New World of genuine co-operation, where everybody has a constructive part to play, that allows the current participants to move forward. And as the Spiritual Light of intervention intensifies, the Life Force available for those who are drawn to lovingly implement the Vision will greatly increase. Conversely, the Life Force available for those expressing violence and untruths of any kind, including rhetoric, will decline substantially.

These fundamental changes in human life are manifesting in small increments - no movie special effects of visually degenerating bodies are expected here. But on a minute by minute, hour by hour basis, individuals will increasingly feel a surge of empowerment as they focus their personal intentions on any aspect of the Divine Plan/Vision of a New World, and this will greatly facilitate its manifestation. On the other hand, those individuals including government and corporate officials (and their operatives), who resort to violence, untruths, and financial manipulation to enforce their preferences, will experience a progressive sense of disempowerment. Even those who practice manipulative control over others to get them to take actions other than for their Highest Good, will experience this diminution of life force.

With this fundamental shift of the parameters surrounding manifestation, each individual seeking to evolve needs to look meticulously at the way he or she conducts their life activities and take corrective action to bring them onto their own Illuminated Path. To listen to their hearts consistently and relegate their mental faculties, however astute, to a subservient implementation role, will enable them to swim with the prevailing current and remain within a sacred space on a continuing evolving basis. Imagine going about one's daily activities and interactions and finding that each person one encountered projected warmth, concern, interest, a sense of common cause, and was indeed fully present in the moment.

Now what would it take to go beyond just imagining and actually manifest such an experience in a society where these values and behaviours are the norm? Although there are some individuals who have always lived their lives in this fashion, most people would probably feel that a major miracle would be required to bring about such a life revolution.

Yet the power of the Cosmic Illumination projected onto the Earth over this decade is so profound that those individuals, who open themselves to this new sacred and magical reality, will truly find a new approach to living. "Life" will support the new approach so fully that, after a while, they will be unable to understand how they ever lived any other way. Subsequent chapters will go more deeply into how to flow with this transition as every aspect of our lives is transformed. The reader will be able to tune in on specific approaches and changes to make within their individual lives, in order to be part of the evolving New World.

It is recognised that for many individuals currently striving to maintain a positive balance within their lives, while living in the current energy environment, it may seem that so much of their life flow is needed just to maintain the present status quo. How are they to find the extra time, focus, and will to initiate such fundamental shifts in their living pattern? To such people the essence of this book is dedicated. The next chapter addresses the process of change – the myriad of alternative thoughts, word, and actions chosen by an individual which aggregate to fundamental life shifts.

CHAPTER FOUR
Opening to Change in Life Experience

The realisation that all situations can be greatly improved from their current status, if the intent is there, is an important starting point. This enables relevant and focused action to be subsequently taken in strength. Many people go through the motions of subscribing to the general belief that progressive improvement is desirable. Yet up to now, relatively few individuals have felt strongly motivated enough to consciously effect significant change and upgrade in their lives, as an objective in itself.

Even when they have a specific desired goal in mind, the protesting chorus of "shortage of time available", "we've never done that before", and "limited resources" in general all too often reduces many people to a state of unfulfilled resignation. In this state, any spark of initiative that an individual does take all too quickly succumbs to the collective gloom emanating from colleagues, family, and friends. In the cause of facing life's everyday reality and staying with what's practical, the doors of potential exploration of alternative options are rarely opened more than a sliver.

Going Beyond Recreating the Past

We all have to go beyond the human subconscious mind's dedication to recreating the past - the repetitious behaviour patterns, the all too predictable automatic emotional responses to situations arising, the often damaging addictive actions of smoking, or eating and drinking unhealthy substances.

For many people, the most suitable arena for mounting an effective conscious challenge to the repetitive subconscious hegemony in their lives is that of diet and nutrition. It is more practical to start by focusing one's conscious will to achieve balance and appropriateness of food and drink consumption by following a committed nutritional regimen, than to attempt to discipline and tame other less tangible automatic patterns of behaviour and response.

Achieving a more alkaline diet, or to consciously substitute some high quality protein for an initially desired sugar-sweetened pastry, is a fine exercise of will, and hones that faculty directly for great future benefit. It also helps one's nervous system calm down on a physical level so that the automatic patterns themselves are less taut and less insistent; thoughts, feelings and actions can happen slowly enough to allow conscious intervention to be effective. We go into this nutritional process more fully in Chapter Ten "Sustaining Health and Wellbeing".

By comparison, it is much more difficult to identify and grasp a complicated emotionally-driven behaviour pattern in another aspect of life and then bring about substantial modification. For example, seeking to modify a habitual drive to continually control and direct all people and situations within reach could be like wrestling an octopus, in terms of bringing about a more conscious approach, without first having been through the previously described wilful honing of nutritional and dietary behaviours, which can lead to a substantial relaxation of the nervous system.

Emotional Release

Having laid the foundation of the balanced and alkaline diet and having invoked the depth of individual will to implement this nutritional Enlightenment on a daily basis, the door is opened to access the old, stored emotions, so many of which yearn to be released. Compressed emotions become more accessible at a component level, where they can be addressed, made conscious and gradually calmed and allowed to depart. There are, fortunately, a range of effective approaches to embracing and neutralising our stored emotions, before allowing them to pass gracefully away into the mists of forgiveness and all-accepting peace.

One of the most powerful resources available for this process is that of Nature in all her Glory. Nature has been described as the manifestation on Earth which is nearest to the Godforce and the Living Spirit. When we walk in Nature or sit in a special place in her midst, a direct interaction takes place between our emotional bodies and the Realms of Tranquillity throughout the various Nature kingdoms. This can precipitate a release on the human emotional level as the individual attunes and aligns with the harmony all around. It is Nature's harmony and tranquillity which absorbs the human emotions available for release quite effortlessly, however jagged they might be. The human emotions pass into an infinite void which remains in stillness.

We learn from Yogic practices about the power of breath to move pain or other discordant energy out of any places where they may be lodged within the human body. These techniques are equally effective with the release of trapped emotions, which can congregate around various chakras, as well as in the muscles and joints. Even without the formal Yoga postures, the power of deep breathing from the abdominal region can be profound, and there are various schools such as Bioenergetics, Re-birthing, and the work of Stanislav Grof which fully explore this approach and practice of emotional release.

At the very least, the reader is encouraged to consciously use abdominal deep breaths at any time to balance out and release any emotions which come to centre stage. We already have a cultural memory of taking a deep breath before beginning a major spoken communication or kicking off with a new line of action. It is recommended that we take this approach a step further and use it to neutralise any of these jagged feelings, which might come up, to assist and enable the Heart-Centre to open and then stay open.

As we breath in, visualise Golden White Sacred Light streaming in, breaking loose, and dissolving the emotions embedded in all parts of the body; on breathing out see the dissolved emotions moving steadily outwards. The initial out-breath will usually be discoloured (almost smoky) but, as the special breath inhalation is continued, the out-breaths will become closer in colour and texture to the original Golden White Light of the in-breath. The exercise should be repeated daily for as long as the out-breath is significantly discoloured. When it becomes similar in colour and texture to the in-breath, then the exercise can be conducted on a more occasional basis instead.

With nervous system responses and emotional flow in relative harmony, a complex behaviour pattern can be addressed piece by piece, with a much greater opportunity to focus effectively on root causes and how to intercede to change their effects. There would also be less risk of the evolving individual experiencing a debilitating descent into emotional chaos if they changed certain patterns, which happened to be critically interdependent with other unstable aspects of their life. This descent could be like a house of cards collapsing, instead of the building of a new structure, step by step on firm foundations.

Creating Your Part of the New World

We have outlined the important process of individuals learning to make sound and lasting changes in all aspects of their lives. This is because the "Creation of a New World" can only be fully manifest on Earth through many people deciding to align themselves with the vast array of changes occurring within the ambit of Cosmic Illumination. The plan now evolving provides for people to create their own individual part of the "New World" and have it harmoniously and consistently merge with others' individual creations to form a flowing illuminated pattern of "New Life".

These individual creations do not have to be expressed as some exotically esoteric enterprise or service, even though some will develop apparently miraculous forms of healing or other practices quite "outside the box". Others will find new ways to rearrange for a Higher Good the Spiritual energy expressing itself in business or governmental fields.

Many others will create their part of the New World by creatively addressing and reforming every angle of their lives. They can look at family and personal relationships, business and professional activity, community involvement, recreation and personal study. In each of these spheres of endeavour, the cause of Spirit and the Light will be advanced by million upon million of small actions and words being re-orientated towards lovingly expressed warmth, harmony, inspiration, creative advance, and all forms of thoughtful cooperation.

In aggregate, these become a major revolution in living energy, an entry into a whole new paradigm of consciously and consistently focused life applications. It is the essence of the new Spiritual Energy impregnating the Earth at this time that, as individuals accept and embrace its new axioms as the foundation of their lives, every part of their lives will indeed re-orientate comprehensively.

New World and Old World: Diverging Paths

Yet freewill as a right and tenet of the human experience is not being superseded by any aspect of the incoming Cosmic Illumination. Some people will choose, consciously or unconsciously, to be unaffected by the new energy environment in terms of their thoughts, feeling and actions. The delegated power and ability of their subconscious minds to control all parts of their lives will continue unabated, faithfully repeating past reactions on a continuing and predictable basis.

While there has always been some divergence between such people and those who consciously take control of their lives by opening to Spirit, the scale of the divergence will escalate dramatically. The various individuals aligning with the new Cosmic Illumination will more and more readily be able to recognise others of the same chosen alignment. They will still be fully participating in daily life on Earth, albeit with a steadily increasing level of Enlightenment drawing them into new arenas of life.

In contrast, the simultaneous experience and viewpoint of those people continuing on the same path as hitherto, will have the tone of "what's all the fuss about", "its all been said before, its just another way of saying it", and "why should I change my way of life, I know what to expect and can handle it". So a New World will grow within and alongside the "old world".

Those individuals who are consciously part of the New World will develop a deep inner sense of knowing with regard to the Realms and Dimensions beyond the physical plane. They are likely to experience a gradual distancing and separation from the "old world" of conflict and disharmony, as more and more of their attention goes to more enlightened creation.

We will continue to develop the more detailed concepts of aligning with the new Cosmic Energy in the primary arenas of life. This will enable the reader to attune to the specific approaches they can adopt and changes they can make in their individual lives in order to align with the growing New World.

A New Golden Age

Over the centuries, many people on their individual Spiritual paths have yearned for a Golden Age when their dreams of a well-functioning, harmonious, and mutually loving world would truly be continually present. For so long it has seemed that it would always remain in the abstract or in the mythical stories of the Golden Ages of ancient civilisations. Now, in this extraordinary time period of 2006-2012, the promise of fundamental change is coalescing at last. The challenge for each individual is to find their way forward to being part of the New World and actually participate in that continuous joy and harmony so long dreamed after.

CHAPTER FIVE
Restoring the Male/Female Balance – A New Spiritual Reality

For the last two thousand years, the Spiritual paradigm of the predominant civilisations of Earth have been overwhelmingly masculine in their overall tone, in marked contrast to those in the millennia proceeding. There was a shift from Etruscan to Roman hegemony of central and northern Italy after 500 B.C. which illustrated the extreme contrast between the two societies. In Etruscan society, male and female genders had a broad equality of status, with an ultimate deference to the Spiritual Feminine. In contrast, the Roman Empire operated a masculine dominated regime, where the ultimate deference was to the successful use of violence. As Lao Tzu phrased it: "However a man of conventional conduct proceed, if he be not complied with, out goes his fist to enforce compliance".

The concept of power changed from "Being the Highest Truth" and "Having the deepest insight", to that lowest common denominator of a great concentration of potentially destructive physical force, with all the associated fear and threats. The Divine Feminine principles of a Higher Good, an awareness of and receptiveness to requests and perceived needs, as well as a fundamental faith in ongoing creativity, were submerged by a landslide of narrow self-interest driven factionism.

As the Romans forcibly subjugated the Mediterranean region, the Light of the Divine Feminine was dimmed throughout. In Palestine and surrounding areas, the extreme masculinisation of the Roman occupation made it difficult for any woman to speak publicly, let alone work with spreading Spiritual Light or inspiring the world with Illuminated Wisdom.

Mary Magdalene was a vital source of Spiritual Power and Wisdom. As Jesus' inspired partner, she enabled the teachings to be felt on an inner level with great power and clarity, even though it was not acceptable for her to teach in public. Unfortunately, the Roman Catholic historians recorded her as a woman of dubious character, in line with their normal priority of putting ideology before truth.

In France and England, the Druidic order of civilisation was fundamentally based on the full participation of women as well as men in government, education and Spiritual hierarchies. The destruction of the Druidic society and the transfer to the exclusively masculine operations of Roman government in all its forms resulted in women being relegated to an observer status at best and, all too often, as subservient participants. This relegation was continued by the Christian religion after the Roman political takeover of the church.

Although the former Druids who had become priests in the new Christian church carried forward the traditions and ethos of male and female equality for a generation or so, they were superseded by others who were inundated with the dry regimen of a masculine and fear-dominated church.

As the Roman Catholic Church grew in political strength and its fear-driven domination of society, it initiated programmes of persecution to prevent women from continuing their own Spiritual activities, in addition to being excluded from the Christian mainstream. The one available path of convent life addressed the Spiritual needs of only a small minority of women who did not wish to participate outwardly in society or have biological families. Spiritual and philosophical education ceased to be available for women who did wish to live an outward life.

The Church laid down their narrow framework of mental and emotional values for other people's lives and exercised violent enforcement to bring about compliance. Although some of the ideals from the early Christians survived for several hundred years in the English Celtic Church, by 900 A.D. most of that Light had been snuffed out by the Roman monopoly. From the perspective of the Divine Feminine, the Roman Empire was the most distorted and destructive period of the last six thousand years of evolution. The horrors of the 1914-18 war, Nazism and Communism, could only manifest because of the suppression of much of the influence of the Divine Feminine presence of Light, Love, and Wisdom during the last two thousand years.

The administrative, legal, and technological skills of the Romans had originally been assumed from the Spiritually evolved Etruscans. In contrast, the Roman spiritual life was a dark void of capricious and vindictive pseudo gods and goddesses, who often shared the narrow mental and emotional attributes of the people who worshipped them.

As the political entity of the Roman state and Empire imploded in the 3rd and 4th centuries AD, the baton of suppression and distortion was passed to the Roman Catholic Church. They greatly magnified the scope of the imbalance (stemming from the exclusion of the Divine Feminine) by claiming to be the only Earthly expression of God, and suppressed with Roman ruthlessness any individual or group with even a flicker of original insight, will, or creativity in any arena of life..

Consequently, when the Roman Catholic Church was challenged and partially replaced by various kinds of Protestant churches, the new churchmen continued with the tradition of the strictly masculine deity. Fortunately for the human race, the newcomers were less able to enforce the rigidity of their views and policies, which led to a considerable proliferation of competing denominations and institutions. But the search for truth was underway, albeit still crippled much of the time by an ignorance of the need for the re-installation of the Divine Feminine as a foundation for greater enlightenment.

The Light of Camelot

One ray of light, amidst all this darkness, was the insertion of Camelot into Southern England during the sixth century A.D., bringing a powerful realisation and manifestation of the natural harmony of Divine Feminine and Divine Masculine. Although most of the stories and myths which live on from that time feature the knights going on their individual quests or banding together to fight outside invaders, an important unreported activity of the ladies of Camelot was to impregnate the land with the Light of the Divine Feminine.

Their success was such that these Light Energies can still be felt and experienced today, within the old boundaries of Camelot, some fifteen hundred years later. Equally importantly, it provided a beacon during the very dark ages of the next one thousand years or so whereby individuals could feel a refreshment, a softening within themselves, when they were in that territory. But, typically, the masculine dominated society after Camelot recorded mostly the stories of the knights' exploits, while the ladies of the court were only awarded supporting roles.

Return of the Divine Feminine

Only since the 1970s has The Divine Feminine begun to move significantly towards its natural position as a powerful source of Light and inspiration, in alignment with the Divine Masculine. In various Western churches, women priests have changed the traditional tone of female exclusion. In the fields of metaphysics and New Age Spirituality, women have taken leading roles as authors, workshop leaders, as well as organisers of whole new Spiritual movements.

These fundamental changes are equally important for men as for women because of the very great need to find ways to create balanced male/female harmonies in every aspect and arena of life. In many activities and occupations, the qualities and characteristics of Feminine Spirituality have gradually penetrated more and more deeply: the nurturing, the receptive, the creative, the all-encompassing, the ongoingness of life, the high valuation set on depth of insight and truth.

As part of this process, it has been vital that women have entered arenas which have historically been exclusively masculine, and equally vital that men have, in varying degrees, opened up to their inner feminine essence.

State of Grace

However, in the next decade, during the run up to 2012 and beyond, the Spiritual and evolutionary changes required of both women and men in terms of opening the Heart-Centre are far beyond anything hitherto experienced, other than on an occasional individual private basis. During this period, some people are going to evolve to a consistent State of Grace, permeating all parts of their lives, as the essence of the Divine Feminine becomes all-present within. The Divine Feminine will contain and balance the refined Masculine Spiritual Essence and, in combination, fill the Inner Being.

Of course, there is still free will, and many people will avoid or side step the strong evolutionary currents flowing towards a State of Grace, as their subconscious minds seek to maintain a state of unchangingness in their lives, striving faithfully to continue to recreate the past. However, the new softer Spiritual environment will enable more individuals to step out of their subconscious addiction.

In those few parts of the world where there is some openness to real change (not just cosmetic change, re-packaging, or an empty gesture), the number of individuals choosing to evolve to a consistent State of Grace, may end up being a significant minority within the population. In most areas, it is likely to be just a few groups or individuals. However, the current purpose of this book and its successors, is to alert the reader to the massive shift of life direction involved in attaining this State of Grace as part of the reinstatement of the Divine Feminine/Divine Masculine balance as the foundation of human life on Earth.

Beyond Intellectuality to Heart Attunement

One of the recurring themes of the New Age is the changing status of mentality and rational thought. During the latter half of the twentieth century, intellectual reasoning has been elevated to almost a theological level in the way it is held and regarded by mainstream society. Even those exercising raw power in pursuit of their own interests, feel obliged to pay lip service to rational justification for their actions and intentions in terms of serving or satisfying some common values of society. But, just as theology was invented and practised by those who could not perceive God directly so, all too often, the practitioners of the intellectual go through their elaborate processes of reasoning, unable to directly perceive the deeper truth of an issue, principle, or situation.

The old tenets of mystical wisdom held that truth always reposes beneath the surface of an issue, principle, or a situation. The challenge for each individual is to learn how to search for and tune in consistently to the deeper, more profound understandings. This process of learning to tune in and probe for the underlying essence is one of the ultimate life challenges for each individual, and requires, as a key essence, the new Spiritual Reality of the Divine Feminine in balance and harmony with the Divine Masculine. When Einstein observed that the average human only used fifteen percent of their brain capacity, he was implicitly identifying the remaining space available which needs to be filled by Attunement with this new Spiritual Reality and associated understandings and practices of Enlightenment.

We can sometimes observe this higher level of attunement and focus between a mother and young child, as they interrelate intuitively and lovingly. In the new Spiritual Reality what is being called for is an extension of this example of close mutual awareness to a broader context; of a heightened state of consciousness and Attunement throughout all kinds of life situations and involvements, for both women and men.

The Path to the Higher Self

The major growth challenge for all individuals on the Path is to learn to attune to their Higher Spiritual Self (who originally thought them into Being and Consciousness) to such a degree that the intellectual and mental aspects of Being become like notes of a well tuned piano, to be played and performed on by the virtuoso Spiritual Consciousness. Within this relationship, mentality can achieve its highest form of expression within pure thought, and realise insights and understanding of the utmost value. The ego shrinks to become but a minor performer (perhaps in the percussion section of the orchestra) while its close associate the subconscious mind becomes an ongoing obedient servant in furthering the causes of the Higher Spiritual Self, manifesting new realities moment by moment.

In this State, there is no longer any scope for the subconscious mind to pursue its favourite pastime of recreating the past ad infinitum. Instead it is focused intently and continuously on realising the causes and creations of Enlightened Spirit and participating in their manifestation. The Path leading to this idyllic state of "Freedom from the Known", as Krisnamurti put it, has been sought for thousands of years by Spiritual seekers in many guises and under many names. Various descriptions of this superconscious state range from Samadhi through Nirvana, The Tao, to finding the Philosopher's stone, the Holy Grail, or (more simply) connecting with the God/Goddess within.

Until recent decades, knowledge and practices used to facilitate progress along the individual Spiritual Path were kept closely guarded secrets, usually available only to successful participants in initiation processes, designed to test the suitability of individual candidates to access higher Spiritual experiences. Qualities of self discipline, tenacity, love-based action, and intuitive perception enabled candidates to pass through the initiation processes and undertake the major courses of study and inner development. Mystery schools, temples, ashrams and similar institutions existed primarily to provide these opportunities to qualifying aspirants, who would often spend many years to just locate the Spiritual school most suitable for their inner susceptibilities, which then might or might not accept them.

As the 1960s progressed, more books began to appear, in clearer language than hitherto, which introduced the reader to some of the initial metaphysical principles of the inner Path to the Higher Self. As each successive decade passed, many such insights came to the surface in the form of assorted publications, workshops, and Spiritual teaching programmes. However, it is only very rarely possible to discover this Path from just reading books, because the one-sided stimulation of the mental faculty does not, in itself, change an individual's relationship to their subconscious mind, or open the connection to the Higher Self. Those individuals who say they have in fact done it all through books, in most cases already had direct access to their Higher Self, but were unconscious of it.

The use of sound patterns, including guided meditations and forms of toning, have been far more effective. The extraordinary range of vibration and pitch attainable through the projection of sound can enable a substantial breakdown of hard encrusted and otherwise ossified emotions and thought forms. The release and freedom so achieved might otherwise take years to bring about through other practices. A crucial common element, within all effective approaches, has been the ability of each individual to open to the unexpected, the unknown, the irrational, and the universal love of Spirit or the Divine. Without this opening, the subconscious mind will edit and interpret every event, incoming communication, and even a surprise event, in terms of what has happened in the past and the various memories of it: mental, physical, and emotional.

In the years running up to 2012, avenues are becoming more readily available for individuals to make an explicit connection to their Higher Selves as one of the prerequisites for achieving Fifth Dimensional Consciousness. As the veils between the refined Spiritual Realms and the Earth plane become thinner and more transparent, opportunities are opening for connection to the Light of the Ascended Masters and the Angelic Realms, in ways which would have been highly improbable even twenty years ago.

If the Spiritual waters are allowed to warm up, the rigidity of an individual's thought forms can melt into a living flow. In an emotionally warmer environment, a Heart Centre can open up and allow the subtle voices of wisdom from the Higher Self Guidance to be heard and felt with more depth and certainty.

A Continuing Connection to the Spiritual

The direct Spiritual awareness and experience, which has been a major part of the lives of a small minority in times past, will become much more readily available to others seeking new ways of living. Instead of having a priest or similar figure to act as an intermediary, an interpreter (and all too often as a controller), the Spiritual teachers and facilitators working with such individuals offer a very different focus of service in helping the new Spiritual seekers to directly access and connect with their respective Higher Selves in a necessarily individual way, and without any sense of competitiveness. Many paths of development can open up and enable individuals to develop a deep and permanent relationship with Spirit.

For those on the Path, the direct connection to the Spiritual will come to be regarded as normal as the conventional abilities to read, write, speak and listen in one's language of birth. This broad advancement in direct Spiritual participation is a vital prerequisite to achieving Illuminated levels of leadership and participation in government, communities, education, business, and health-sustenance.

During this period of broad transition in every sector of society and life itself, there will be a diverging co-existence between institutions of the old kind and the new Spiritually-integrated holistic forms and structures, attuned to the inspirational energies of the Angelic and Spiritual Realms. In the remaining years up to 2012, the cosmic energy of change flowing through and around the Earthplane will enable and ensure that the Spiritually-attuned organisations and groups will grow steadily stronger. Meanwhile, the old style structures will become more dysfunctional and somewhat disempowered.

Divine Feminine and Divine Masculine in Balance

In the context of this major Spiritual Infusion, what will it take for a harsh symbol like a traditional Christian cross to be replaced by the softer feminine symbol of the Chalice or Holy Grail? At present, only a few British and Breton churches use the mystical Celtic cross which combines male and female energies in a balanced way, expressing the very ancient metaphysical symbol of the crossed circle. Here, the feminine circle contains the masculine mystic cross, with flowing branches of equal length, a symbol appropriate to the new Spiritual Attunement of Fifth Dimensional Consciousness.

In the Spiritual realms, the Divine Feminine and Divine Masculine are continually aware of which respective energy input is going to advance a situation to its Highest Realisation, and they divide up responsibilities and actions accordingly. A similar approach to co-operation and synthesis is required on the Earthplane, with an overall focus on attaining the highest evolution in every part of human society.

So one of the most profound and deeply acting waves of change is rolling through all areas of human endeavour. This is enabling the new Spiritual Reality of a true balance between Divine Feminine and Masculine to take fertile root in all receptive beings, groups, and organisations, within the framework designed by the Angelic Realms and Ascended Masters.

CHAPTER SIX
The New Attunement of the Heart

In the previous chapter, we touched briefly on how mentality and rational thought had, in the public perception, substantially replaced traditional religion as the resources of ultimate truth. For mainstream society still, it is within the practice of rational reasoning that the answers are usually sought when dealing with religious and philosophical issues of "rightness and wrongness", of truth and falsehood, and of moral justification for a course of action.

The change in approach and belief required during the run-up to 2012 and beyond is far more radical than the previous major paradigm shift from traditional religion to rationality. This previous shift involved moving from various sets of somewhat rigid mental-emotional religious beliefs to even more varied patterns of rational beliefs. The transition addressed the way in which external circumstances were being regarded as the basis for many assumptions about everyday life.

Over the next few years, the metamorphosis available to Humanity will be in the profound re-orientation from the predominantly externally focused mental/rational paradigm to a Heart-related inner perception and experience of individual reality. This will encompass an inner universe of unlimited dimensions, rather than the miniaturised arena of external perception where one is literally seeing and interacting with just the "tips of icebergs".

Much contemporary communication is so shallow and inaccurate that ongoing misunderstandings are a normal state of affairs for the individuals involved. Participating in any groups, the misunderstandings would be compounded without limit, as we witness all too often in contemporary societies.

The current mass-consciousness is all too easily maintained by media strategists with their shallow and constantly changing targets for external commentary, which defy any insight in depth. The common characteristics of this mass-consciousness are vagueness and inaccuracy, as individuals jump from one diversion to another, without either the tools or the inclination to probe the inner content.

The New World of Heart Focus

By focusing through the Heart, an individual can begin to access a New World, a multi-dimensional arena where experience and consciousness relate to the present moment. From a Spiritual perspective, this is an infinite moment, containing simultaneously within it the energy from all the pathways leading up to that moment, as well as being a foundation and starting point for the paths leading away from it. The phrase "worlds within worlds" directly relates to this microcosmic viewpoint, from which all other worlds are accessible.

Through this access, it is feasible to experience in a clairsentient way the full range of qualities within a particular world – the texture, the sound, the colours, the scents, the emotions, the predominant beliefs, the constraints, the humour, the electricity of life, and, certainly not least, the expression and flow of Love.

This ability to be intimately involved in another world, accessed through the Heart, goes far beyond a mere intuitive insight or a gut feeling. This might be compared to a virtual reality video guided tour of a house, contrasted with some quick snapshots of the outside.

When we talk about focussing or connecting through the Heart, we are referring to the involvement of the Heart chakra and the physical thymus gland, rather than the physical heart. The physical heart is strongly influenced by the energies flowing or not flowing through the Heart chakra, but the physical heart is not in itself the means of connection. Other names which relate to the Heart chakra are Heart Centre and the Etheric Web of the Heart, which aptly describes this ultimate multi-dimensional "broadband" connection of unlimited "bandwidth".

The energies flowing through this infinite portal enable Heart-feeling level connections to facilitate interactive communication across an unlimited spectrum. Involvement, harmony, illumination, supportive co-operation, a sense of holistic well being, can all become normal characteristics of living on such a continually focused basis. A State of Being opens up where Attunement with Universal Truth enables each individual to share themselves and be part of the whole. They are able to offer from their personal world to that collective State of Being what can fit harmoniously, and to receive, accordingly what fulfils their true needs.

Alignment with Love and Spirit

For an individual reaching these levels of Attunement, the ability to participate broadly in life increases exponentially without external limitation. The process of Attunement as the basis of decision is an integral part of utilising Einstein's "other 85%" of the brain, the part not used by the average person.

This is indeed a supersonic piece of computing compared with the relatively cumbersome nature of intellectual thought and debate. Attunement uses the insight of intuition, but takes it to a higher level by aligning one's consciousness with the full spectrum of all present Love-based Spiritual realities.

A group composed of individuals at these levels of Attunement may live what might be termed a magical existence or a charmed life. It is however, the conscious Attunement, which is the enabling factor in this State of Being.

The Power of Clear Intent

So what exactly is the process of connecting through the Heart? How does an individual start to attune with their Heart Centre? How can they access and eventually continually align with the New World within? As with all successful endeavours, the starting point is to have a clear intent. It may be difficult initially to be both specific and detailed in one's intent to open and attune the Heart, without having previously experienced this condition to some extent.

A sincere intention and commitment to make a permanent shift in one's life orientation, by entering the inner worlds, is sufficient to attract the attention of helpful and evolved teachers from the invisible worlds of Spirit. As W.H. Murray of the 1924 Scottish Himalayan Expedition put it so eloquently in describing the power of commitment:

"Concerning all acts of initiative and creation, there is one elementary truth, the ignorance of which kills countless ideas and splendid plans: that the moment one definitely commits oneself, providence moves too. All sorts of things occur to help one that would not otherwise have occurred. A whole stream of events issues from the decision, raising in one's favour all manner of unforeseen incidents and meetings and material assistance, which no man would have dreamed would come his way. Whatever you can do, or dream you can do, begin it now! Boldness has genius, magic, and power in it".

The setting of the great intention to commence the vital process of learning to connect through the Heart, will reverberate throughout the human subconscious mind, and activate previously dormant programmes, macros, and subroutines designed to open up the Heart Centre. Going beyond this initial stage, the vital next step is a clearly spoken intention and a request to the world of Spirit. A series of spoken affirmations in the present tense will facilitate the continued opening of the Heart Centre, through physical changes in the endocrine system and energetic shifts in the Heart chakra itself.

The Power of the Spoken Word

The emphasis is strongly on using the power of the spoken word to achieve the desired opening and a connection to all Spiritual Realms of Light. In these days of massive interpersonal communication, it is easy to forget that the spoken word was originally used to create reality, rather than just communicate it.

The opening words of Genesis "In the beginning was the Word, and the Word was God" relate strongly to this understanding. As the affirmations are spoken clearly on a daily or preferably twice daily programme, the opening up of the Etheric Web of the Heart edges forward:

> *"With each breath, my Heart Centre opens to the Luminescent light of Spirit";*
>
> *"I am connecting through my Heart Centre to the unlimited essence of the Living Spirit in all her forms."*

Other Disciplines to Open the Heart Centre

There are other quite different and important approaches to changing the body's vibrational Attunement so as to enhance progress in opening the Heart Centre. Some that are most widely practiced are: Yoga, Tai Chi and Chi Gun, and Sufi-based practices such as Zikr and Dances of Universal Peace.

The inspired use of breath, movement and sound, (in various combinations) within these disciplines, has a profound effect upon the body's subtle channels, including the Heart Centre. The reader is invited and encouraged to choose such of these activities that feel enlivening to them, since there is no one approach which works best for everybody. Rather, it is best to feel the path and practice you are most drawn to – maybe it feels familiar in some way, however irrationally.

Having found one or more of these practices with which to attune and implement, it is of critical importance to participate fully and regularly, despite all the protestations of one's subconscious mind. This feedback may include (but is not exclusive to):

"I don't have the time to do this daily."

"It doesn't really make much difference whether or not I do this practice."

"My partner/family/friends think I'm crazy and antisocial spending so much time doing this."

It is important to keep in mind continually that the Law of Cause and Effect provides an objective result for a given amount of action. There is also a great cyclical strength in emphasising inclusion of an activity each and every day. Hence, to optimise progress in opening the Heart Centre, a daily practice of 20-30 minutes will work well. An additional longer practice several times a month will make it all work even better.

Good Nutrition Helps Heart Opening

In the context of our review of the various approaches to expedite the opening of the Heart Centre, it cannot be overemphasised that good nutrition on a regular basis is a vital and necessary foundation upon which to build. Good nutrition in this context, means an abundance of nutrients needed by all body systems, which is considerably more that the minimum necessary to just prevent immediate adverse symptoms of malnutrition, infection, or malfunction of an organ or gland.

There needs to be an ongoing conscious assessment of what specific nutrients are necessary for each individual and from what sources they are being received, whether from food, drinks, or supplements. Building a strong nutritional foundation for daily living will bring many benefits of sound functioning of the physical body, an effective immune system, and increased personal life energy available. This higher level of body functioning will also facilitate the opening of the Heart Centre by permitting an inner silence in which subtle sounds and feelings are more readily perceived.

Role of Energetic Healing

A fourth approach towards the opening of the Heart Centre is to find a Spiritual healing practitioner who undertakes chakra and aura cleansing. There are a variety of different approaches from various schools. Some are from well known schools such as Reiki, Barbara Brennan, Berkeley Psychic Institute, and various derivatives and extensions of each of these. There are many other individual teachers and practitioners who choose to maintain a local profile or even anonymity. See which practitioner or teacher you are drawn to once you have declared your intent to connect with the healer, and who appears to be most aligned for you and your desired Spiritual growth.

A common element within all these energetic practices is the ability to speed up the opening of the Heart Centre by removing the dead or stale energy accumulated in and around the heart chakra like a crust. For most people, the opening will be broader and deeper if a variety of energetic healing is experienced, and if each of the chosen treatments types are undertaken in a sequence or a phased rotating basis, rather than simultaneously. All these treatments would be well complemented by sessions of therapeutic massage and acupuncture to help deepen the energy flow.

Time for Opening the Heart Centre

It may take months and possibly years of process and treatment using all the approaches described in this chapter so far to significantly open up the Heart Centre:

** *the setting and expression of the intention*

** *the energetic body movement practice*

** *the diet and nutritional programmes*

** *the spiritual healing and cleansing*

The good news is that, with the heightened and more refined energies available during the next several years, the process of opening can be achieved in profound depth, provided the intent and practical focus are maintained.

The opening of the Heart Centre is a multi-dimensional process and must be worked with as such for optimum results. In a not dissimilar way, an archaeological excavation of a precious ancient treasure like a mosaic pavement has to remove all material covering the whole area, rather than just being content with a narrow shaft sunk vertically. Just as the opening process is multi-dimensional, so is the process and experience of being totally present in the fully opened Heart Centre. This is the ultimate system of connection with living energies in multiple worlds. The qualifying condition for such connection is having compatible ranges of wavelength frequency. These ranges can be extended, deepened and upgraded by ongoing practices including those described earlier in this chapter. The more the Heart Centre is opened, the broader the range of wavelengths which can be engaged with.

One could draw comparisons with the internet in the physical world, which has been a major evolutionary step for mankind compared with the simpler and more tangible communication methods of previous epochs. But the internet operates on much narrower wavelengths of words, pictures, sound and numerical data. It is restricted to these energy patterns and, implicitly, the emotions, physical actions and other responses induced by the receipt of such internet communications. But it does share with the Heart Centred communication the great flexibility of connection.

By comparison, whole worlds can be experienced in depth through the Heart Centre, with instantaneous interactions and embrace. The energies of love, caring, humour, illumination, causational explanation, evolutionary understanding, can all be experienced in depth directly throughout the Etheric Web connecting all Spiritual Realms. The contact is instantaneous, although there are often time-lags as an individual tunes into the appropriate wavelength for the desired interaction. For example, by "going deeper" in a meditative state, individuals have felt a sense of opening up to the whole universe.

For an individual to evolve to Fifth Dimensional Consciousness during the crucial run-up to 2012, their ways of living and functioning on Earth need to upgrade to a level where a normal, everyday way of operating is indeed through the Heart Centre, in all its multi-dimensional and "unlimited band width" essence and content.

We are talking here about a revolution of such a profound scale, that it will indeed be the "Creation of a New World". We will look in more detail at how this Heart Centre revolution will transform all the social and governmental institutions around which external human life revolves and interacts: interpersonal relationships, business and the workplace, education and enlightenment, health and well-being, governance and the competition for power. But above all this book is dedicated to showing how each individual can fully participate in this revolution. In the most practical ways, an individual can invigorate every part of their life and living experience by being in-tune with the new Heart-based energies -- the new standard in the post-2012 world.

The Strength of Spiritual Support

Many are aware that individuals living on Earth have attempted and struggled over the centuries in their search to find a way to reconnect with the Light within the Heart Centre. It has often been hard to reconcile the aspiration to reconnect and the seemingly dark void full of great obstacles in the way. What is different now is the great Spiritual Support available and manifesting for those individuals aligning with the Light. As well as affirming that they truly wish to be part of the New World of Heart-based reality, they are willing and committed to putting their will, working time, and resources towards this cause.

The effect of the Spiritual Support may sometimes appear to be quite subtle in its effect – the indications of a changed outcome may seem to be a stage or two removed from the original focus. A significant change may be identified as having transpired, yet there will no reason apparent for it having come about at all, let alone coming about with relative ease. On a personal level, it may seem that the environment within which one is working becomes more responsive. Apparently unconnected events happen which recalibrate the various factors in a business equation, yet always one's will and intention must be maintained at full strength.

Despite the profound change in the energy environment described above, the collective human memory of the previously unsupportive world conditions lives on, and can act as a misleading influence on choices being made in the here and now. This collective memory can act as a drag on a person's willingness to take what appear to be substantial risks in their life, to go out onto the proverbial "limb".

To begin to develop a new confidence that "things can work out well this time", and that an individual's powers of perception can grow to a long-term level of enhanced Illumination, it is suggested that an attitude of wilful experimentation be adopted. Initially, the key is to maintain modest expectations, while following the four approaches to opening the Heart Centre, described earlier in this chapter. As the practice deepens, it is more straightforward to go into the Heart Centre and try out new connections to Spiritual Light.

As the warmth of these new connections is experienced and internalised, a new regime is established within, containing important elements of faith, understanding, continuing access and opening to a New World. This new inner pattern directly affects what manifests in all outward aspects of human life, in every field of endeavour and experience. The open and Illuminated Heart Centre may prove to be a veritable lifesaver as the changes around 2012 become more intense.

CHAPTER SEVEN
The Rising Tide of Human Consciousness

Starting in the year 2000, Light Energy has flooded the Earth plane, and the realms of human awareness, with the specific intention and goal of achieving Fifth Dimensional Consciousness comprehensively by the Winter Solstice of 2012. According to Pythagorean numerology, 2012 is a "five vibration" year which, symbolically, is a year of transition within the recurring nine-year cycles.

The year 2012 is scheduled to be the Mount Everest of transition years, since individual years began to carry number vibrations. The changes to be completed are apocryphal in their scale and depth of penetration. All individuals will experience some level of cataclysmic change in their lives compared with their personal expectations as recently as 2005, which may come to be seen as the last "normal" year of the original paradigm.

Some people will reach sublime levels of inner joy and Spiritual connection, while others will have found themselves unable to live and breathe at the growing Fifth Dimensional Consciousness. They may choose to move out of physical form and leave the Earth in favour of a more suitable planet, one which matches their existing level of vibrational consciousness.

The concept of a rising tide of Higher Consciousness illustrates how the new paradigm of understanding and relationship will penetrate the very fabric of life on Earth. This Higher Consciousness inevitably and inexorably will cover and penetrate every square mile of the Earth's surface.

Individuals Separated from the Light

Those beholden to the old third dimensional beliefs and life practices of materialism, separation from Spirit/Higher Self, and continually lusting after power and self-aggrandisement, may have been able to avoid the rising tide of enlightenment for the last several years. However, from 2006 onwards, the islands of high ground where they can hide or retreat to will become smaller and ever fewer. By 2012 the new vibrant, joyful, colourful, heart-centred, sea of love will have penetrated every place and being on Earth.

The experience and condition of those who choose not to learn to swim in these refined waters, might be compared with that of an individual losing their sanity, almost as if a discordant high-pitch "sound" inside their head rises in pitch and volume. Nothing in everyday life would seem to make sense in any familiar way, and the old ways of behaviour and predictable cause/effect patterns simply would not compute any more.

Many of those aligned with the old ways will be unwilling to respond to these stimuli to seek new avenues of changed living patterns. However, some individuals at least will pull away at the "eleventh hour" from what will have become more and more an untenable way of being, (or more accurately a living death) and make a start on learning and adjusting to the new paradigm. Left to this late stage, it will be rather like climbing a near vertical slope without mountaineering gear, but a few individuals of great willpower, clear intention, and the foundations of Heart warmth can make real progress towards the new Cosmic Enlightenment and associated vibrational frequencies.

Schooling for Spiritual Awakening

During the next several years, Spiritual schools of varied kinds will be making themselves readily available for individuals realising at least that "life" is changing in some subtle but important way, and that they need to be part of the change. The Spiritual Hierarchy has emphasised that the decision to be made on an individual basis is whether to join the "Rising tide of Consciousness" and be part of the "New World", to decide not to be involved, or to be totally unaware that there is any decision to be addressed at all. Substantial resources and facilities for development of Consciousness will be available for those in the first category choosing to be included.

The Diverging Paths

As the diverging gap between the old and new ways widens, there will be a rolling manifestation of new communities living at the higher and rising frequencies. They will seem to be in the same physical world as the old order, yet actually becoming more and more separate. Land and buildings from that old order will become more available, as individuals choosing not to release the old ways find it increasingly unattractive to stay incarnated in physical form on Earth, and hence move on to other realms with more suitable living conditions for their needs and level of awareness.

With less competition for productive land, it will become more feasible for those attuned to the new frequencies to come together to form vital self-sufficient communities based on the land and buildings of old estates or traditional farms, whose land has not been contaminated from the decades of mainstream chemical farming.

The Shifting of the Poles

Another development which will facilitate these sweeping changes of land use and settlement, is the shifting of the North Pole from its present location in the Arctic to somewhere in the Himalayas, close to the legendary Shamballa. This dramatic anti-clockwise angular movement of the land masses will have the effect of moving the British Isles and Western Europe closer to the Equator, with a related angular effect for North America. Conversely, much of Asia will move further away from the Equator. The Southern Hemisphere will change correspondingly as the South Pole moves West and North. Some areas that were formerly cold and unsupportive of cultivating crops will become warm, temperate and fertile.

At the time of writing, the higher temperatures at the poles have already been observed objectively, and they are having direct adverse effects on the local inhabitants, of both human and animal species. However, as the process continues, a more positive outcome will be observed in Scotland, as it becomes as temperate as the present climate of Southern England. Wild land, which up to now has been used mostly for sheep grazing, will become suitable for careful cultivation of fruit, vegetables and grains on ground uncontaminated by chemical fertilisers.

Similarly, as Canadian winters become warmer, more Northerly areas can be used for organic or similar horticulture since they also have not been contaminated by industrialised agriculture. More generally, some areas that are currently little more than desert, can be brought back to fertility, as the local climate becomes more temperate.

Some of the most dramatic consequences of the angular movement will manifest from the greatly accelerated melting of the ice caps in both Arctic and Antarctic areas. This will restore the Earth to a spherical shape, which is a prerequisite for the establishment of a more consistently temperate climate on Earth, post 2012. The melting of these ice-caps will release a huge mass of water into the oceans causing a significant increase in sea levels up to 20 feet, enough to inundate the coastal areas of habitation in many countries, including some major centres of population and economic activity. Since a large number of these cities are primarily located at sea level, whole city populations are facing the loss of their urban and waterside habitats.

Changes in Financial Systems and Control

Another major consequence for our current world would be the decline or demise of most of the world's major financial centres located in those principal cities close to sea level. As those vulnerable financial centres go under (in both senses of the phrase), their control over the world's economies and its inhabitants will be substantially reduced. Financial instruments and the paper currencies, based on the printing press and unlimited credit liquidity, will give way sufficiently to enable new trading units to be selectively established, based on the real value of gold, silver and/or local systems of barter and exchange.

These new trading systems would make a substantial contribution to restoring local community control over systems of exchange. Governments and banks would be restricted in their ability to create and extend their purchasing power by printing money or its equivalent electronic process, literally producing money out of thin air.

It is an unfortunate truth that most of these financial centres are controlled by individuals devoted to unlimited acquisition and retention of personal wealth and power, without concern for the consequences of their actions on Humanity as a whole. However, as the power and influence wielded by these individuals and their financial institutions diminish, a sense of lightening up will increasingly be experienced by New Age pioneers, as they push ahead with their self-sufficient communities. These will be founded in previously little used areas and based on an affirmation of Oneness with the Light. The dedication of these communities will help and sustain the evolution of our beautiful planet Earth as she evolves into Fifth Dimensional Consciousness.

PART TWO

THE EFFECTS

CHAPTER EIGHT
Relationships, Family, and Community

In an ideal world, the Attunement of the Heart would be at the functioning centre of relationships of all kinds, and particularly those of a personal and family nature. Even relationships primarily of a business nature (including some marriage relationships) take on remarkably different qualities of warmth and deep mutual understanding when they are based on the Heart Attunement.

Instead of individuals stumbling around as if blindfolded, and occasionally making real contact when they bump into one another, with the Heart Attunement a more continuous connection is in place. This enables intimate contact on a variety of joyful wavelengths.

If these wavelengths were represented in terms of their colour vibrations, the resulting picture would be quite similar to various abstract mystical artists rendition of themes such as Bliss, St John's Revelation, the Joy of Spirit etc. Through the subtlety of the hues and the seamless blending of different streams of colour, these show the extraordinary range of energy and meaning available through the Heart Centre. These are readily available for the communication of thoughts, emotions, and complex realities.

In marked contrast, if an individual's Heart Centre is closed, the quality of communication and interaction attainable in a relationship is adversely affected, because the only wavelengths available are of a rather coarse vibration.

The Subjective Meanings of Words

The use of the mental faculty, instead of the Heart Centre, as an alternative primary focus is fraught with the risk of great confusion and distortion. It is most unfortunate for those who depend on the use of words, that the latter do not have clear and precise meanings, let alone meanings which could be termed unique.

Yet how can it be that even with the use of complex dictionaries, so painstakingly compiled by linguistic experts, words often do not have the desired clear or precise meanings when they are put to use in spoken or written sentences? It is vital to understand that each person's actual "installed dictionary" which they access, consciously or unconsciously, each time they speak, write, read or listen, is unique in its content and assigned meanings. This uniqueness reflects and incorporates the individual experience of word usage for each person. Our personal dictionaries build and evolve throughout our lifetimes, and it must be realised that the meaning of a word, as we hear, speak, or read it, is the sum total of all the previous occasions in which we have experienced that word.

When we exchange words with our fellow humans, in what we believe to be the same language, in fact there is a wide variation in the extent of shared comprehension resulting. Naturally, individuals who have spent long periods living together (or at close quarters) are usually going to have the greatest common ground when using words to convey meaning. The greater the contrast in life and word usage experience during the formative years of building the individual vocabulary and "installed dictionary", the more challenging is the task of communicating with words without ongoing ambiguity.

Our personal inventory of words is indelibly marked with the emotional contexts in which the word has been spoken, written, read or heard. This might be just a few times or maybe several thousand times. Each time the personal use of a word is re-experienced, the indelibly marked emotions surface and significantly mould the meaning experienced and/or projected in the new usage.

Communication without an Open Heart Centre

Even if our personal "installed dictionaries" and emotional memory of word usage were, against all the odds, reasonably standardised, communication using words alone would be quite inadequate as a means of conveying concepts, images, and feelings, which are essentially non-mental. Even those verbal languages which are more suitable for expressing those feelings are hard put to convey more than our proverbial "tip of the iceberg" of a concentrated emotional state.

So, beyond words and lacking an open Heart Centre, an individual can resort to physical touch (or be the subject of it), and also project and receive sexual and emotional energies at the second and third chakra level (related to the power of attraction and the gut-level reality/perception), with strong overtones of power and control.

Physical touch does provide some means to convey a variety of feelings, but these are still heavily skewed to a more down to earth kind of interaction, usually one with lower frequency vibrations. In fact, in order to utilise the higher frequency vibrations of physical touch, it requires an open Heart Centre to facilitate the subtle tuning necessary, as a concert pianist relates to the piano keys or a Spiritual healer passes the subtle vibrations through their hands to their clients.

It is in literature that one can readily find plausible examples of characters of these various levels of this Heart openness and, rather more often, of Heart closedness. To find a good example of an open Heart Centre, one may go to Jane Austen's Eleanor in "Sense and Sensibility". She had an ongoing sense of the direction she and her family needed to be heading. She innately knew, as her sister (Marianne) lay on her death bed after losing the relationship with her loved one (Willoughby), that her appeal for her sister to stay living on Earth, would be received in her sister's Heart Centre, despite her sister being indefinitely unconscious.

In contrast, to find a character who communicates totally on a mental or intellectual level, E M Forster's Cedric in "Room with a View" provides a graphic example of that type of restriction, limitation, and inability to be able to perceive beyond the superficial phenomena of the present situation, often making references back to a mental data base for the attachment of meaning.

King Edward 1st of England, immortalised in the film "Braveheart", provides a prime example of an individual who, devoid of any Heart Consciousness, operates predominantly through third chakra qualities of untempered power and control, backed up by the coarsest levels of expression of physical touch, indeed of ruthless violence.

Many Levels of Heart Openness

In real life, people have and experience many levels of Heart openness, when it comes to relating to others. Opening the Heart Centre is not a linear transition from "closed" or "partly closed" to "open". There are many layers within the Heart Centre and, indeed, centres within centres. Even when the Heart Centre is predominantly open, there can be pockets which are unevolved and show themselves but rarely. They coexist side by side with the higher frequency vibrations of an otherwise open Heart Centre.

This is, for example, the underlying cause of Spiritual leaders who, after years of relatively pure and attuned living, suddenly have an apparent relapse, taking an action which seems to be totally out of character, when one of these un-evolved pockets is activated. This activation then provides an opportunity to upgrade this aspect of living energy and character to a higher frequency level, with the associated behaviour of that level. But it is only an opportunity, and the ongoing tendency of the human subconscious mind to want to recreate the past, can sometimes abort an individual's attempt to upgrade to those more refined levels, particularly when aided and abetted by negative encouragement from the astral plane.

A Deeper Heart Connection

The Attunement of the Heart enables a much deeper connection to be sustained in all interpersonal communication. We go beyond just depending on the use of words, with all the ambiguities arising from each person's individual understanding of words, phrases, and sentences. As we have seen, this is based on personal, and often quite different experience of word usage, coupled with all the emotions associated with those past situations. It is important to hold the truth that the meaning of a word as we hear, speak, or read it, is the sum total of all the previous occasions in which we have experienced that word. We can then consciously open our Hearts to bridge whatever gap there may be with the other person's total word reality.

The open Heart Attunement allows a vital element of softness to permeate a stream of spoken words – the warmth and wisdom for the Heart Centre will modify and overlay every part of the communication. The softness and warmth from the Heart Centre will touch every sentence, every paragraph written, uttered, read or heard. The ambiguities of words will be modified and overlaid by the clarity of the Heart vibration, not unlike the effect of uplifting music in a dramatic film, which enables the audience to perceive a higher meaning and deeper feeling from a character's speech.

For the person who uses the medium of physicalness as a prime means of expression in life, the intermingling of the softness and warmth from the Heart Centre with each physical action and contact results in a Higher Consciousness expressing itself within their physical world. The previous examples of the concert pianist and the Spiritual Healer's hands are overt examples of this Higher Consciousness expressing itself in a readily visible form.

Less dramatically, there is enormous scope for small, tender physical expressions of this Higher Consciousness. These might be a gentle touch on a shoulder or face, a warm hand shake, a handwritten note of a joyful and loving nature, a hand-crafted gift, a beautifully prepared meal to share with others, and a consciously cleaned room or dwelling – shining with the loving energy used in the process.

Fifth Dimensional Wave Communication

As we evolve further into Fifth Dimensional Consciousness, verbal communication will gradually be replaced by "wave communication". In this way, whole multidimensional concepts, pictures, desired actions, outcomes, and deep understandings are transferred in an instant between individuals at the level of inner knowing. As Fifth Dimensional Consciousness prevails, what has hitherto been the preserve of Heart-opened intimate couples and Adepts, will become the universal mode of communication, independent of knowledge of any verbal language. And the Spiritual, emotional, mental and physical environments will increasingly support this enlightened way of being and interaction until it feels truly normal. We go further into wave communication in chapter thirteen: Education as a Life Experience.

We have given these examples of the effects of an open Heart Centre on communication and interaction to illustrate the dramatic changes which can be brought about in every aspect of living. The potential for real change in the world is colossal, as more people manifest this state of profound inner consciousness within themselves.

A Lightness of Social and Business Relationships

One of the most potent arenas for the dynamic expression of this inner consciousness and awareness is in relating to other people at any social, business or family level. As the Heart Centre energies blend seamlessly with the mental, emotional, and physical bodies, a new lightness becomes a normal presence in both casual and committed relationships.

This can occur both in an informal interaction at the supermarket checkout to the deepest involvement at all levels between two individuals. We go beyond the ongoing confusion and misunderstanding, which is the inevitable state of human relating in the absence of a fully engaged Heart Centre. Instead, a predominant tone of harmony and trust prevails as a normal state of living and interacting.

Not surprisingly, there are day to day, week to week, and month to month variations in the level of collective harmony, rather like the ocean swell rising and falling, constantly finding new shapes and textures. But from the perspective of the individual, as well as looking at society at large, it would be a calm ocean, rather than one with raging storms and giant, potentially overwhelming waves.

We are describing here the consequences of a revolutionary change in the human experience of being and living on Earth. This is not some mere incremental improvement, but a permanent step through a doorway to a New World, for those who choose this path and then do what is necessary to walk down it. Naturally, there would still be growth within the process of relating in general as well as participating in specific intimate relationships. It would, however, be a growth of the experience of Heart-Centred living, wherein new levels, new colours, new tones open up to deepen an individual's ability to relate, and express joy and truth in so doing.

It would not be necessary to continue to experience the hard knocks and bruising experiences of relationships based on physical attraction, emotional co- dependency, mental idealism and illusion, and the general tendency of the human sub-conscious mind to recreate past relationship situations again and forever, until a person gathers all their will and focuses on an expression of "enough and no more".

Family Relationships

Relationships within a family context are equally open to being transformed through the process of opening up the Heart Centre. Family relationships are a special case within the general energy patterns of relationships, which we are in the process of examining. In families, relationships are usually played out over a much longer period, which results in greater accumulated complexity as one layer of experience interfaces with another, quite often in a partially incompatible overlay.

As these layers accumulate over years and decades, the buried incompatibilities react, commonly in a repeating pattern, but sometimes, quite unpredictably. Either way an event or series of events come about which are largely determined by the embedded patterns from the past. Multiple dimensions of expression are added to this mix with the involvement of all the members of the family. Analysis of group dynamics provide an opportunity to look at the manifestation of incompatible interfaces for each combination of family members.

However, to change the interactions requires the involvement of each member of the family in being willing to take the step of opening their respective Heart Centres. In so doing, all can grow to that State of Consciousness where they are simultaneously aware of being part and parcel of each other's existence, whilst still maintaining a strong sense of individual awareness. As we have seen in other contexts, it is through the Heart Centre's openness that the universal energies of love, generosity, and mutual understanding can become the normal currency for family interactions also.

Neighbours and Communities

These patterns and interactions, which underlie family behaviour and its potential evolution to a higher plane, are just as applicable to living with neighbours of all sorts. It applies to interactions between inhabitants of a village or similar small community, within a city or country, just as much as with the folks in your street.

However, a major difference between the family energy expression and that of the larger groups is that the individual memories of interaction are replaced by a group's mass consciousness, based on a pooling of individual memories of interaction. In the process of this pooling, many of the memories become changed and sometimes distorted: sometimes through misunderstanding, sometimes because the true recollection is too painful to sustain, and sometimes through deliberate falsification by individuals seeking power and control, who need a specific "history" to sustain their dark doings.

Pooled Memories of War and Martyrdom

A recurring example of these changed collective memories is that around wars that are "won" by a particular country. The pooled or group memory gives heavy emphasis to the heroism and gallantry of the country's warriors (both survivors and war dead), and to the implied moral and cultural superiority which resulted in the victory. The physical, mental and emotional suffering of the Armed Forces participants in the fighting is downplayed substantially, together with that of their families and friends. This is to enable the dominant paradigm of heroism, gallantry and "it was worth the sacrifices to achieve victory" to prevail.

A similar example is the use of a group, who suffered death and degradation at some point in the past, being converted into martyrs. Here the specific intention is to use the memory of their misuse to pressure other groups or nations to grant them special privileges subsequently. These exemptions from natural consequences are demanded, even if the other group or nation has had no involvement at all with the original harm inflicted on the "victim" group. The pooled memories are exaggerated and distorted by those wishing to manipulate and distort using the leverage of victimhood.

However, the expediently modified collective memory for that particular country and/or victim group will adversely affect its relations with other countries for an extended period because of the untruths and imbalances unconsciously feeding into the diplomatic interface. Since each country has a potent mixture of distorted collective memories across a wide spectrum of arenas (not only war-related) the scope for incompatible overlays is both varied and extensive. History is full of the buried incompatibilities reacting with each other, all too violently.

New Inspired Approaches to Collective Relationship

Fortunately, some new approaches in inter-country and inter-community relations have flowered in recent decades, which are more related to such Heart-Centred concepts such as inspiration, idealism, the hand of friendship, and empathy.

One of the more innovative of these approaches has been the "twin town" and "sister city" programmes in Europe and North America. In these fresh connections, a community in the one country develops a direct relationship with a community in another country, with emphasis on cultural and education exchanges. They share understandings of what contributes to the creation of a thriving community. They go on to develop multiple ways in which collective friendship and co-operation can actually be implemented, rather than just talked about. By focusing on the "here and now", instead of the historical national stereotypes, these direct contacts can step beyond the distorted memories and incompatible overlays from the past.

What can we learn from the success of these "community to community" direct contact programmes about lightening up interactions within villages and towns or indeed, within families? Establishing new channels for contact are part of a universal key to going beyond the collective relationship patterns of the past which allow the open Heart Consciousness to take centre stage. Within larger urban areas, this could be moved along by more direct connection between individual households in different parts of town. In a smaller village, it might be the devising of occasional assemblies with a representative available from each family. For a family, it could mean members finding different ways to regularly experience each other in an informal, positive, lively and cheerful context.

As these new modes of contact are experienced, the involvement of the Heart Centre deepens, the accumulated memories of the subconscious mind are held in abeyance. The newness of the different kinds of human interaction avoids the involvement of the automatic memory access of the subconscious mind, which all too often gets in the way of experiencing the present situation in real time. And the cause of community, in its broadest concept, is advanced by all these new Heart-based connections.

CHAPTER NINE
Aligning with Universal Abundance

In recent decades, a great deal of creative attention has been addressed to the ongoing challenge of achieving material prosperity in a world where scarcity and lack are believed to be quite normal characteristics of human existence.

As we go deeper into the exploration of universal abundance at this phase in the evolution of our world, the keys to opening up these fundamental energies will be found in various approaches to the Inner Way. The age old mystical understandings of manifestation illustrate the need for an individual to go within themselves to create the foundations for whatever conditions in the outside world they wish to bring in to being.

The understandings relate to a much broader arena of human living than just the physical actions of acquiring assets, resources and income. They include the higher aspirations of growing in heartfelt sensibility, a generosity of Spirit, a delight in the expression of beauty, and a fuller and deeper experience of all life. As the Spirit becomes more recognised, accepted, and consciously present in an individual's life, the manifestation of these higher aspirations will be sought and desired as fully as the physical conditions and attributes of daily living.

A Heart-Centred Approach to Abundance

As the Earth moves steadily toward the Fifth Dimensional reality of 2012, a Heart-Centred reality becomes desirable and indeed, more practical. The traditional approaches to obtaining resources, through physical effort and mental complexity, will quite rapidly diminish in effectiveness and viability, unless they are linked to an inner Spiritual awareness and manifestation practice. Those individuals choosing to stay with the outward-facing traditional approaches will increasingly experience the phenomena of "spinning their wheels", a feeling of losing traction as much effort produces less forward motion.

People, who have settled for an unchanging position on the "treadmill" of basic living, will find it more and more difficult to sustain their repetitive patterns. Seemingly, they will put out more and more effort for less and less return. The concept of "plan your work" and "work your plan" will fade into oblivion, unless the vital stage of building a Heart-based Spiritual foundation of inner inspired creativity is inserted as a vital foundation.

As an individual's Heart-Centre opens, there is a gradual shift in their interests, desires, and relationships to the dynamics of human life on Earth. Since it is through the Heart that we become aware of the Illuminated Invisible Worlds, there is a natural shift of emphasis in an individual's engagement with life, away from the purely physical/emotional experience, so typical of third dimensional consciousness and its daily expression.

A fundamental change in an individual's relationship with life comes about from the inner realisation dawning that they have an ongoing choice whether or not to enjoy a situation, an interaction, or indeed any experience, by the exercise of their own Will. Instead of the subconscious mind reacting to an outside stimulus and coming up with a response of assessment and judgement based on recalls of similar stimuli in times past, the Heart reaches out proactively to contribute warmth, Light, creativity, joy, appreciation, empowerment and similar qualities.

A shift of great significance has taken place in an individual when the nature of an experience is determined, not by the reaction of the subconscious mind to perceived events or situation, by an open Heart Centre directly connected to the Enlightened Realms of Spirit. The individual maintains a state of warmth and happiness at a Heart level and handles all that comes up in life from that place of Light.

Developing Community Abundance

A noticeable consequence of this shift will be the de-emphasis of personal possessions reserved predominantly for private individual use in favour of sharing the utility of resources with groups of like-minded others, with a common purpose. This leads to a much more efficient use of resources and is one of the foundations of a functioning community. Naturally, this does require that the groups of like-minded individuals need to find practical ways to live close to each other, so that they can effectively support and share in joint projects.

It is suggested that this conscious choice of community by attuned individuals and families is much more suitable for Attuned social organisation in the years leading up to 2012. This should supersede the more traditional patterns of going where your job or profession seems to require or finding the house you want to live in and then learning to co-exist with the inherited neighbours, with whom there is only a narrow range of shared interests around just being in that location .

With the land and sea alterations resulting from a major change in the Earth's rotation pattern around the Winter Solstice of 2012, a new environment will be created where "civilised survival" will represent the major level of abundance individuals will seek to manifest. This will be a far cry from the unfocused conspicuous consumption, particularly of the last ten years or so, which has been to a large extent a searching for self-gratification by appeasing the emotional desires and demands of the ego. Yet the relief experienced by an individual was usually very short-term, and the individual operating in this mode would spend much of their leisure time seeking for the next shopping expedition and/ or acquisition to maintain this emotional respite.

In the next phase of life after 2012, Heart-based community abundance will readily encompass the ongoing manifestation of food, housing and clothing, as well as tools, equipment and materials for small scale production of the simple necessities for life in physical form. The sources of the provision will change and become more varied as Fifth Dimensional Consciousness opens new portals. As has been pointed out, this low-key approach to the fulfilment of tangible human needs will take place naturally within groups and communities, where individuals pool their skills, resources, and energy for the satisfactory maintenance of all participants.

Abundance through Joyous Celebration

The open Heart Centres of each person open the door to unlimited planes of enjoyment, where loving, creative expression is the primary and ongoing experience of living, even in the face of physical adversity. Although this Heart-inspired expression is felt as an inner joy on an individual basis, there is also a sense of group celebration appertaining, which is greatly enhanced by the practice of sacred music, dance, and other related forms of expression. This sharing of Light energies through open Heart-Centres enables even the smallest and simplest task or contribution to take on a joyous quality. This neutralises any emotional sense of a burdensome workload, although the body can still reach a state of physical extension, after which rest and rejuvenation are still most welcome.

When there are no overtly positive or negative events, no divide between "fun" activities and those of a "work" related nature, the individual can experience a critical step into the Light and a profound sense of freedom and release. Instead, the enlightened individual maintains a flow of loving warmth from their Heart-Centre, adjusting the frequency to balance and strengthen each situation being addressed and experienced. The subconscious mind and all its memories of past stimuli of pleasure derived from specific actions, places, products, sensations, and anticipations, is relegated to a useful but subsidiary role of calm remembrance, with the former third-dimensional complex of emotional motivations confined to archival records. These can, of course, be accessed for a Heart-orientated storytelling , where the energy flow is derived from the Heart Centre of the narrator, and the old memories become merely its raw material.

Heart-Based Communities

At this stage, Humanity's higher creative endeavours will focus on the expression of community-based enterprises to further development of advanced environmentally low-impact technology, and new understandings of light, sound and relationships with nature. This evolved whole life purpose will then be so far removed from the "Age of Materialism" that the latter's memory will fade into the same oblivion as war, pollution, and central banks.

The good news is that we can now choose to move decisively in the direction of this new Heart-Centre paradigm and begin to plan, provision and construct the new communities of Fifth Dimensional Consciousness. Given the major rearrangement of land and water around 2012, suitable locations can be chosen for these communities which are not currently valued very highly or sought after competitively in the current and expiring "Age of Materialism". Even before land is acquired for these new communities, Heart-Centred people can come together and create relationship, activities and experience to lay the Fifth Dimensional Consciousness foundation for the future of humanity.

Individual Change and Manifestation

Having aligned with the changing needs of the years prior to 2012, the individual seeking on a practical level to abundantly pull new experiences, new awareness, and/or new resources, must allow themselves to feel all the various strands and components of whatever it is they are seeking to pull to them. This starts with scanning comprehensively around that which is desired. One must become aware of all the emotional connections associated with the goal – the hopes, fears, disbeliefs, worries, expected relief, or indeed the possible delight.

Concerns may come up as to what extent friends and family will be accepting of the individual once the desired change has manifested. Reactions of worry, fear, and disbelief in their own capability may come up. Even though they may acknowledge that others can make this kind of transition successfully, a doubting individual may ask themselves whether they can pull it off themselves, whether they can integrate this change into the rest of their character and habitual way of life. They ask themselves "Will I have to modify other parts of myself and my life to function compatibly?" And on top of all this, "How can I find the time to undertake all this change anyway?"

If these concerns were left to be addressed on just a mental level, the mind would no doubt automatically think each issue to death, without reaching resolution. In contrast, holding each concern within even a partially open Heart Centre, and asking for Spiritual Guidance and Angelic help, an individual will be enabled to find a meaningful perspective which can be felt simultaneously on multiple dimensions.

As each strand, each part of a situation is felt consciously at the Heart level, it becomes more straightforward to fully accept them, thus clearing the path for the desired change, awareness, acquisition, or move. Alternatively, at the Heart level, one might feel that a particular strand or part of a situation is undesirable to a significant extent. If so, it's back to the manifestation drawing board to reassess and refocus on what one really wants to create within the Fifth Dimensional Consciousness context. This is a situation where all the strands and parts must feel like they can be consciously embraced as personally desirable and appropriate within the overall framework of an evolving Earth. Then each of the new combinations of strands and parts can be held in Heart Consciousness to ascertain the degree of acceptance. This validation process within this initial phase continues until all the parts are cleared, and the desired balanced objective can be manifested with an internally unobstructed flow.

The second phase requires Belief to be breathed into the creative project that is coming into manifestation, even though the individual creator does not know wholly or even in part how the project will actually come about. It is the nature of Belief, and its relatives Enthusiasm and Excitement, that it brings into clear focus energy structures which exist in the alternative vibrational frequencies of thought and aspiration. Because of the inevitability of Belief bringing into focused manifestation those energy structures which it irradiates, it is critically important to go through the procedures of the first phase of testing and sorting outlined above, in order to eliminate any unwanted strands or parts. Otherwise, any of these remaining can destabilise or distort the final energetic pattern which materialises.

An important corollary concerning the manifestation of physical objects or structures is to visualise, create, and project belief in a generic sense for the exact conditions which one wants to bring into one's life, rather than focus on a specific item or solution which is currently attached to or owned by another person. The manifestation process attracts resources which are unattached to another person's projection of use and/or ownership. Even if they are still owned by another, it is important that the other person has released them – for example, by consciously putting them up for sale without regret– so that they are energetically available to the next user.

It is an eternal understanding that there is no limit to what can be manifested as long as one does not restrict the source of the supply by saying "It's got to come from here" or "It must come in this way". It's important to be able to accept satisfaction of the need or want through a completely unforeseen solution.

At the opposite end of the manifestation spectrum lie fear, hopelessness, despair and sometimes angry emotions around the lack of desired conditions in an individual's life. The essence of belief works objectively to bring these unabundant aspects into focus and hence manifest physically their effects and consciousness for as long as the belief is maintained, consciously or unconsciously. The subconscious mind dutifully works away at recreating the past in this context also until the individual, by an act of conscious will, replaces and overwrites the old memory and its associated belief. Holding the desired new situation in the Heart Centre softens the rigidity of the identification with the conditions existing within the original pattern. It allows hope to grow that some change "might" be possible and opens the door to beginning the initial phase of manifestation described earlier in this chapter.

However difficult and challenging that we may have found this whole process of releasing the past and energising the manifestation of what is really needed and desired, it must be emphasised that the cosmic energy environment is becoming lighter and less dense. A process which, in the past, may have required almost a Herculean scale of application to achieve even a modest level of fresh manifestation and change, now can flow more freely, particularly if the process is practised consistently on a regular basis and help is requested directly from the Spiritual Realms.

The importance of each individual becoming consciously aware of their own ability to bring about their renaissance of manifestation cannot be over-emphasised. Bringing about profound change in the world of mankind and evolution to a

Fifth Dimensional level of abundance requires that each individual persistently addresses their own challenge in a dedicated way.

The third phase is to move into (and stay in) a state of thankfulness for everything that manifests each day, both physical and non-physical, and for all that is in the process of manifesting through the first two phases of manifestation. One can also include thankfulness for all the beauty, warmth, joy, and abundance and so on that is in the process of manifesting about which one knows little or nothing in advance. These qualities are being drawn continually by the warmth, love, and joy within one's Heart Centre.

The actual act of giving thanks aligns the individual with an unlimited flow of Light energy, which induces an altered state of being. Here, giving and receiving are simultaneously part and parcel of the same action, within an overall State of Grace. Within this timeless arena, the classic third dimensional cause and effect sequence is transcended into an unending stream of positive moments of creation. Within this stream, all manner of inspired manifestations become possible.

The suggestion is being made to approach the process with deeper understanding, using the three phases of manifestation outlined in this chapter. As the evolution of the cosmic energy environment provides more and more support, an individual can consciously change their orientation towards a strong personal belief in their natural ability and deservedness in manifesting any particular item or situation, and all that is necessary and desired in a more general context.

It is further suggested that each individual learns to manifest in the most conscious way possible, fully aligned with the

Spiritual Realms without any sense of dependence on an outside physical source for their ability. And as more individuals learn to live in Spiritual abundance and alignment as a normal everyday way of living, as whole communities adopt these principles and practices as their modus operandi for all arenas of life, a massive shift of focus takes place to return power to the individual, as well as the communities of these strong individuals. This will result in significant changes in the way Enlightened society organises itself in alignment with the Spiritual Realms.

It's important for each individual to consciously get underway with their own personal practice, if they are not already so engaged. The effect of even a small group of attuned individuals able to manifest freely is quite disproportionate to their numbers. The transition of life on Earth to the Fifth Dimensional Consciousness requires these practices to consistently become the normal pathway through each day for those involved, thus enabling major societal evolution to take place. As an individual moves clearly into Fifth Dimensional Consciousness to match the vibrational level of the evolving Earth, the availability of abundant flow can facilitate such instant manifestation as might be regarded as miraculous in other times.

CHAPTER TEN
Sustaining Health and Wellbeing

Most human diseases have a root cause of unsuitable nutritional intake. This often manifests as a weakening and undermining of the body's immune system, closely linked to the thymus gland and Heart chakra. This is complemented by weakening and reduced functioning of other parts of the body, which have not received enough essential nutrients over an extended period. After a certain level of weakening is reached, the body is wide open to an infection taking hold. Alternatively, there may be an outright malfunctioning of a previously weakened organ, gland, or other body part. In both scenarios, remedial nutrition can fill the original omissions, and provides specific rebuilding resources for those parts of the body in need.

Apart from an interest in weight loss, the beliefs of modern health services in and around diet and nutritional needs tend to relate to the needs of infants and young children, or for specific disease conditions like Diabetes, to the extent that they are applied at all. For most of the population, the concept of daily calorie consumption (literally the heat generated in digesting solid and liquid foods) is regarded as a sufficient measure of nutritional intake, truly another "tip of the iceberg" approach.

Unfortunately, very little accurate information about desirable levels of nutrients is available from regular medical sources since nutrition is not taught in regular medical schools in the UK and

USA. It is recommended that Naturopathic doctors or other professionals focusing on Wellness and/or Spiritual nutrition be consulted in person or through their publications to obtain this vital information in detail.

There are many approaches to sound nutritional practices for the purpose of creating a sustained healthy body and Spirit. A common priority is to ensure the full functioning of the immune system and that all body systems have the necessary ingredients for their unrestricted operation. The reader is encouraged to explore several approaches and make their own choices.

The author personally found great value in the work of Dr. Julian Whitaker of Newport Beach, California and of Dr. David Williams of Texas, both of whom publish valuable newsletters and books. Their work is based on a blend of objective third party research and their extensive clinical experience. They include in their understandings the influence of emotional health and the power of prayer. We recommend both their general and specific approaches to building (and rebuilding) well founded health through wise nutrition.

Contrast of Allopathic and Traditional Medicine

The allopathic medicine of contemporary Western society uses a radically different approach from the wisdom and understanding underlying health practices used on Earth for several millennia previously, even though many of the practitioners have a real desire to help their "patients". The mainstream current practices of treating symptoms rather than causes, leads to a high rate of repeat occurrences of illnesses from any particular source, and repetition may involve new and varied patterns of symptoms.

This scenario contrasts markedly with the practices and wisdom underlying health practices in advanced civilisations of the past, which were primarily addressed towards maintaining a complete and natural state of health, as well as immunity to infection or other damage. Disease symptoms in an individual were rare and the prime focus was on maintaining a healthy functioning of each individual. With this focus, and successful follow-through, it was unusual to experience serious imbalances which actually contributed to actual physical symptoms of disease. Practitioners would give much attention to guidance concerning achieving emotional harmony and a healthy nutritional balance to eliminate causes of disease, as well as treatment on the nutritional and physical levels to alleviate and heal any physical symptoms.

In this arena of health and well-being, it is important to understand more fully how and why systems and organisations come into being if we wish to comprehend fully their current functioning. By seeking out and identifying the motives and related objectives of those participating, we can obtain insight at all levels. And we can ask ourselves: "Are the outcomes a balanced "win-win" or a lopsided "win-lose" situation?"

A good example of health practices in ancient times is that of the village physician of "Old China" who knew each family directly as well as what was going on in each person's life. He was able to perceive and work with any emotional imbalances within a household, before they manifested as physical symptoms in any household member. If, despite his intervention at the emotional level, symptoms of physical imbalance or disease did appear, then he had accurate inside knowledge of the root cause and could treat both cause(s) and symptoms directly with great effectiveness. His remuneration was only received while those under his care were healthy. So his financial motivation was wholly aligned with the interests and needs of the village households under his care and protection. This was a true "win-win" dynamic.

The contrast with current Western medical practices and procedures is extreme. Much of the population is sick to some extent on a regular or continual basis. There is an immense commercial business of pharmaceutical drug distribution and hospital surgery serviced by a vast array of personnel trained in administering these treatments, all in all consuming some 10-15% of National Income.

Pharmaceutical Suppression of Symptoms

A visitor from afar might suppose that, with such an enormous commitment of resources going to health services, the population would be extraordinarily healthy and fit. But the reality of repetitive illness, rising epidemics of heart disease, cancer and Alzheimer's, and stressful overload amongst medical personnel all tells a rather different story.

Although there are many dedicated medical doctors, nurses, and support staff trying to make the system function, the never-ending flow of repeat patients (many of them in significant pain) indicates that many of the end-user needs for a healthy life are not consistently being met. The level of frustration and stress amongst the medical personnel indicates that a lot of their needs are not being met either. This is pretty much a "lose-lose" situation so far.

General practitioners involved in the initial stage of diagnosis are typically allowed only 5-10 minutes with each sick patient – just long enough to identify some symptoms and prescribe the specified drug response from the pharmaceutical company's codified regimen. These few minutes of interaction are totally insufficient to identify root causes of ill health. However, since the current regime is content to just address the patient symptoms, there is sufficient information to maintain the flow of pharmaceutical products through the distribution system.

Without an accurate and fundamental recognition of the cause of their condition, the unfortunate patient will set off on an often circular path of suppressing symptom after symptom, only to have the original cause continue to express itself in new ways. The toxicity of the drug treatments often lead to substantial liver damage or even liver failure. The further along this unfortunate path of symptom-suppression the patient goes, the harder it is to identify the original causal imbalance which precipitated the original symptoms.

So we have the current human tragedy of a steadily increasing prevalence of many diseases and conditions, which are generally unresponsive to pharmaceutical responses in terms of effecting a full recovery and cure for the patient.

To sustain the system's credibility, many of these conditions are described as "incurable", yet many decades of research by highly qualified medical researchers have identified and successfully applied nutritional (and other) remedies for these same "incurable" diseases , including cancer and Alzheimer's.

Not only have they demonstrated their effectiveness against the disease itself, but they have provided clear proof of the absence of the disease amongst groups consuming the required nutrients and, conversely, the repeated occurrence of the disease amongst groups whose diet excluded the identified nutrients.

A Definitive Cure for Cancer and its Suppression

The definitive cause of cancer was finally established by the brilliant medical researcher Paul Krebs Jr. in California during the 1950s and 1960s, building on the work of European pioneers going back to the mid-19th century. The presence or not of Vitamin B17 (Laetrile) in people's diets was shown by Krebs to be the definitive factor in causation as well as a highly effective remedy when reintroduced to a patient's diet.

According to Philip Day's book "Cancer: Why We're Still Dying to Know the Truth", this was followed up by five years of successful field trials at the Sloan-Kettering hospital in New York under the direction of Dr. Kanematsu Sugiura which conclusively proved that Laetrile was highly effective in the treatment of cancer.

However, the medical establishment, saw fit to publicly deny the established effectiveness of B17/Laetrile, and with the help of the pharmaceutical lobby, persuaded the US Congress to make it illegal in the United States, which was followed up by major States like California. While Laetrile treatments are freely available in other countries, it is outside the mainstream advice dispensed by general practitioners, so most cancer patients and the general public never hear about its availability and efficacy.

Although surgery can bring temporary relief to a cancer patient's body, it does nothing to address the original cause, which will often precipitate more cancer symptoms subsequently. The great post operative challenge for most cancer patients is surviving the implementation of chemotherapy and radiation treatments which have little, if any, causal effect in terms of curing the cancer, yet have a devastating effect on the functioning of the human body and Spirit.

All this would be difficult enough even if there were no viable alternative treatments. But as the truth emerges that effective causal cures for cancer have been known and quietly used for over 30 years, people will begin to ask fundamental questions about what kind of political-medical system would suppress this vital, much sought after knowledge for the purpose of financial gain by the pharmaceutical business sector.

From Suppression of Competition to ...

It is in the best Roman political and religious tradition to suppress competition from people and institutions with alternative values and understandings. In this context, freedom of choice in the health markets have been greatly restricted, or even eliminated. Legalised monopolies have been established and maintained by force and coercion to prevent consumers and patients from exercising freedom of choice in an open market, on any kind of level playing field.

A New Dedication to Healing

Like other energetic hangovers from the Roman tyrannies, these distortions will change out of all recognition as the influence of the returning Divine Feminine and the fast rising Cosmic Energy environment restores balance within the field of health and personal well being.

As the months and years go by, through 2012 and beyond, the new Energies will support all health practitioners, whose primary dedication is to enable the healing of their clients to take place at a deep causal level, and in this way to naturally eliminate the symptoms of disease. This support will be available for practitioners from all traditions who have this dedication, including those working in Allopathic medicine. Simultaneously, treating the symptoms with nourishing relief is a humane and loving way for a healer to take care of their clients.

Part of the new Heart-Centred Attunement with Spirit for health-practitioners, is knowing that abundant income will follow the practice of excellent healing. Respect for other healers' skills, talents and approaches is an integral part of an overall rationale for a holistic health service, which can comprehensively and effectively address all aspects of attaining and maintaining human health.

The dedication to their client's wellbeing as well as a professional understanding and valuation of the work of their fellow healers will enable practitioners to practice according to a Higher Wisdom in undertaking their own healing treatments, as well as referring clients to other relevant practitioners to enable all aspects of the healing process to be completed.

Individual Responsibility for Sustaining Own Health

In a huge change of emphasis as we enter this new period of enlightenment, individuals will take responsibility for building and maintaining their own health, rather than just ignoring it most or all of the time, until some part of the body malfunctions sufficiently to get their occupant's attention. Spiritual clarity can be greatly aided by having a fully functioning physical body in full vibrancy.

A major component of individuals learning to take a personal responsibility for their health is to develop an understanding of nutrition and its consequences for health conditions (or otherwise) in the human body. This needs to be implemented to such a degree that each person is conscious of why they are eating or drinking each item consumed. This approach does not in any way preclude an ongoing enjoyment of food and beverages, It does, however, require a broader wavelength of pleasure and appreciation beyond indulging in a sugar-rush or luxuriating in the richness of some creamy delicacy.

A conscious awareness that the day's nutritional requirements are being addressed in a specific and relevant way, by whatever foods are being consumed, is a vital step to nutritional health, while still appreciating the full spectrum of taste, smell, and texture. This will enable the appetite to be reprogrammed to permanently align important nutritional needs, eating and drinking pleasure, with physical and emotional satisfaction.

Nutritional consciousness, practiced consistently, will greatly reduce any propensity for the body to malfunction physically. It will endow a firm foundation upon which each individual can build an ongoing vitality and longevity.

It is of outstanding importance that all health practitioners develop both this personal firm foundation in their own lives, as well as a good understanding of the uses of nutritional therapies in remedial contexts. The more they develop a personal practice and insight for themselves, the better they will be able to serve their clients. There is great value in the practitioners leading and instructing by personal example and demonstration of positive and effective nutritional consciousness.

Classes and support groups help to combine the actual nutritional learning and understanding with the sense that it is absolutely OK to make significant changes to eating and drinking patterns, so many of which are linked to social and family rituals.

Within the class or support group, individuals can develop new social and interpersonal associations to link with the practice of the nutritional programme for the new era and for the new consciousness. By allowing the changed way of feeding oneself to be in a framework of an adventure, rather than some kind of deprivation or penance, Illumination and fun can mix together with supportive companionship.

In chapter six, the importance of healthy personal nutrition was introduced in the context of being a prerequisite for the opening of an individual's Heart Centre. The same approach of developing a coherent understanding of the causal connection between nutrition and the healthy functioning of the physical body is recommended as a normal approach to living one's life fully and without physical restriction.

This understanding should be developed to such an extent that an individual's first and natural response to any symptoms of physical disease is to adjust food, drink, and nutritional supplement intakes, increase rest and sleep, and spend time in calming and nurturing environments.

In many instances these responses will be sufficient to return the individual's body to fully balanced functioning without further intervention. It is important to recognise that the responses made relate to alleviating potential and actual causes of the symptoms experienced, rather than seeking to eliminate the symptoms directly.

On the other hand, a situation may be experienced where there is little or no change in the pattern of symptoms despite the implementation of the initial responses outlined above, and the body continues to display imbalanced functioning in various ways. At this point, the individual can consult a nutritionally savvy health practitioner from the informed perspective of having implemented certain responses to the symptoms of disease with a clear and accurate record of what changed and what did not. This naturally enables the practitioner to hone in with much more certainty on underlying causes of the condition.

Emotional distress needs to be uncovered, revealed, healed and released because it is so often a major factor in the origin of many body imbalances. Opening the Heart-Centre as described in Chapter 6 will enable a long term cure for emotional distress. The emotional tension and wounds can be healed by being overlaid by the Spiritual Light and Love condensing through the Heart Centre.

There is a multi-dimensional interaction between physical healing, emotional healing, nutritional enlightenment, and an open Heart Centre. In their interdependence, there is not just one place to start; however, the applied wisdom of excellent nutrition has positive effects along each of the above dimensions, as well as for improved memory and mental clarity.

Guidelines for Excellent Nutrition

Naturally, there are a multitude of approaches to achieving excellent nutrition and, most certainly there is not just one diet which encompasses all needs. There are, however, certain themes which are common to all diets and nutritional supplementation programmes which lead to that desirable state of excellent nutrition.

The most important foundation is the continual intake of spring water or water from a household supply which has been thoroughly filtered. Around four pints of water a day – eight large glasses, will provide the body with sufficient resources to keep glands and organs sufficiently hydrated, to keep the digestive system and intestines functioning well, and to enable the body to flush out toxins and waste products.

The absence or shortage of water causes the body to make unattractive rationing choices between depriving this organ or that process of sufficient fluid for its correct functioning. Although the body control systems are ingenious and creative in allocating scarce water supplies, the long term effect of insufficient water will include ageing and degeneration of the body, as well as loss of energy for living life to its fullest.

The next most important common aspect of the various nutritional approaches, which lead to excellent nutrition, is that of maintaining an appropriate acid/alkaline balance within food and drink intake. A traditional Western diet is heavily acidic from its heavy proteins, most grains, and traditional teas and coffee. The rather sparse leavening of mostly alkaline fruit and vegetables still leaves typical diets with 80-90% acid content – far removed from the ideal ration of 80% alkaline and 20% acid content.

Even many vegetarian diets, not withstanding the real intent to eat healthily, are still far more acidic than the 20% goal. Rice, legumes, coffee and Indian tea, cheese, eggs, lentils, and many beans are acidic and need to be balanced by four times the quantity of alkaline foods and liquids. In particular, great emphasis must be placed on the consumption of raw, uncooked fruits and vegetables, along with unsweetened herbal teas.

Another high priority, both for vegetarian and non-vegetarian diets, is the elimination or severe reduction of refined sugar, gluten (including white wheat flour), and refined salt. In many respects, these substances have even more disadvantages than eating red meat itself, so the elimination of these highly refined items is an essential part of the nutritional overhaul required to achieve optimum health and well-being.

There is also a great need to avoid food contaminated with chemical fertiliser, insecticides and growth hormones, to the greatest extent possible. Unfortunately, even organically produced food is rarely completely free from the chemical contamination percolating through the air of the countryside and the ground waters beneath. Having said that, it must be emphasised that organically-produced food is light years ahead of the chemically produced alternative (even without genetic distortion) in terms of nutrients delivered and a low level of contaminants.

People sometimes say that they would be open to consuming more organic food "if only it didn't cost so much". It is important to realise that in terms of the real cost per nutrient contained, organic food is at all times less expensive than the chemically produced alternative. For example, an organic orange contains of the order of 40-50 milligrams of vitamin C, compared with as little as 5 milligrams from the chemically produced version. By any value comparison, it is worth paying twice as much for the organic orange – the cost per nutrient is up to 90% less.

Without a predominantly organic diet, most individuals are not ingesting the minimum daily vitamin and mineral requirements set out by government health departments, let alone the considerably larger daily amounts actually needed by most people living with the level of air, water, and food pollution typical throughout the industrialised world. During the transition period through to the post-2012 times of freedom from pollution, most individuals will need to support their diet with vitamins and mineral supplements, in the most natural forms obtainable, forms which the digestion can recognise as clearly food-based.

Since hunger perceived by an individual is at least partly in response to the human body's need for nutrients, there will be less inclination to eat a larger amount of food when living on an organic type of diet and/or one with a comprehensive range of supplementation to fill any nutritional shortfalls.

While it may be true that many people are partially motivated to eat by sheer emptiness of the stomach, or by sugar and salt addiction, the effect on most people of consuming nutrient-full food, is indeed to eat significantly less, usually after a transitional period. Much of the Western world's obesity epidemic would disappear if only people followed the broad nutritional recommendations set out in this chapter.

Eating smaller amounts of easy to digest food with a high nutrient content and, separately, drinking abundant amounts of clean water, will enable the body and its components to function well in the long-run with minimal deterioration, just as they were originally designed to do.

Nutritional Supplements and Body Rebuilding

Most people are not ingesting the minimum daily vitamin and mineral requirements set out by government health departments, let alone the considerably larger daily amounts actually needed by most people living with the level of air, water, and food pollution typical throughout the industrialised world.

While it is a great step to change over to eating a healthy diet, the years of eating inadequately have left in most people a legacy of nutritional deficiencies that have caused the body to bypass or even shut down certain bodily functions as originally designed. This is a coping mechanism in order to survive the shortage of necessary nutrients with the least amount of damage being caused to the body. To bring these affected parts of the body back to full functioning, a programme of vitamin, mineral, green algae, and energy food supplementation is desirable.

Combined with a stream of nutrients extracted from organic or similarly pure food, the body commences a rebuilding process which gradually brings the whole body back into balance and fuller functioning. As this is repeated consistently each day, a continual renewal and rebuilding process takes place.

After a cleaning out of old garbage, both physical and emotional, the body engages in a long term restoration programme in which all parts are brought back to their highest possible level of operation. Provided other issues described in this chapter are addressed, the long term path of degeneration and decay, known as ageing, can be avoided or greatly mitigated.

Depending always on the degree of environmental pollution surrounding an individual, and on how little or how much emotional and physical stress there may be in their lives, it is possible for the human body to re-attain the ability to receive and assimilate all the nutrients it requires to sustain life processes without degeneration, from just food and water intake. This would require residence in an unpolluted area with healthy and vibrant Nature energy in immediate proximity, as well as a personal living situation where calmness, creativity and purposeful activity are part of the normal curriculum for each day.

Transcending all the physical characteristics of food, water, and environment, is the vibrational essence of Spiritual Energy – sometimes described as Lifeforce – contained within all beings, and all substances. As we examine the challenge of sustaining health and well being within the human race, perhaps the largest gap in understanding among governmental, medical, and pharmaceutical organisations, as well as the mainstream population, is in awareness of the Living Spirit within all things.

As an individual eats, drinks, and breathes, all that they take in passes on this vital Spiritual Essence according to the vibratory level pertaining. Similarly, as a human touches or is touched by another being, or is exposed to a particular energetic environment, the Spiritual energy within them is directly affected.

Each living being whether human, animal, vegetable, or mineral has its own specific range of wavelengths within its "Beingness" and this is transmitted, received, or shared during consumption or contact. This exchange of "invisible energy", is a little similar to the process of electro-magnetic induction which can be observed in a physics laboratory, however, the wavelengths are much more subtle – even Kirlean photography and related techniques only pick up a sub-set of the total vibration. So our health is directly influenced by the sum total of all the energies we are in contact with whether food, drink, air, or physical and emotional environment.

CHAPTER ELEVEN
The Evolving Workplace

With the re-establishment of the balance between the Divine Feminine and the Divine Masculine, each individual is coming face-to-face with the tremendous God-given opportunity to greatly accelerate their personal and Spiritual growth in the fields of work and profession.

As we move further towards living a Heart-based reality as a key to Fifth Dimensional Consciousness, our attitudes, motivation, and relationship with the worlds of working activity are going through a major paradigm shift. An understanding of abundant flow replaces the old parameters of scarcity and shortage, along with its associate "hard work". Each attuned individual uses their Heart-Consciousness as a means of aligning with their Path of Highest Destiny in order to consciously choose on a continual basis their enlightened steps forward in business or professional activity.

This Path resembles a flexible tubular energy field pulsing with Light energy of many hues, denser towards the centre of the tube of Light, more translucent on the periphery. This is far removed from older concepts of a straight-line vector down which one advances at a predictable pace. New working situations can be dreamed into existence, which contain a balance of exhilarating challenge along with a sense of warm satisfaction from the practical engagement of inspired creativity.

An exceptional degree and quality of interpersonal relations with customers, colleagues, and suppliers naturally provides joyful food for the Heart and Soul. Working activity at this level is a dimension in its own right to be explored and fully experienced within the uplifting and inspiring nature of this energy field, related to an individual's Path of Highest Destiny.

Charting the Way Forward in One's Career

For some years, individuals searching for the way forward in their working career have been advised to carefully reflect on all the various functions, responsibilities, and interfaces with which they have been involved. They should then home in particularly on those parts that they remember fondly for a sense of warm satisfaction, or maybe for an element of excitement.

Alternatively, they can recall a time when their creativity was successfully stretched in coming up with a solution to a new or unprecedented situation. Some of these parts might be valued for the challenge of dealing with a system of great complexity and fully mastering it. Other situations will stand out because of the exceptional degree and quality of interpersonal relations with customers or colleagues.

Whatever the recollection, it is vital to gather up all these warm, positive, exhilarating, creative and innately satisfying experiences and combine them into a valued composite essence. A new focus and framework for working activity can be perceived, containing a high proportion of these valued past experiences. Thus, a questing individual can home in on their Illuminated Path of Highest Destiny.

A New Source of Working Inspiration

As the energy of the Divine Feminine penetrates and restores the Earth plane with ever-growing intensity as we move towards 2012 and beyond, people will find that the exercise of identifying and collecting together all these positive aspects of the working situation is a vital part of moving forward on their Path. Henceforth, it will not be an option to stay entangled with the uninspiring roles from the past, disconnected from Heart Consciousness.

One's whole occupation will need to be resonant with the pulsing Light energy of the Highest Path; otherwise the work flow energy would slow down, dissipate, and disperse – with the individual's working function gradually coming to a halt. This phenomenon has already made itself known in the final decades of the twentieth century, sometimes with titles like Chronic Fatigue Syndrome" or, more simply, "a Burnout". Sometimes it is observed more generically, as when an individual unexpectedly leaves an apparently successful career and goes off "in search of their soul".

The lessons and work/study habits acquired by so many students in the past at traditional schools will become increasingly unworkable in the next few years. Practices like learning by rote and/or learning a skill or profession merely because it is expected to be remunerative, rather than because of a heartfelt attraction, will become totally unworkable. Similarly, having a prime motivation in life of just avoiding punishment or hardship will lead to total dysfunction.

The importance of nurturing the Soul at all times, and certainly in the workplace, is vital and needs to get more prominence within that admixture of an individual's motivations, where mental concepts jostle with emotional yearnings to satisfy the self gratification urges of the ego self. These urges are very often substantially at odds with the Path of Highest Destiny emanating from the individual's Spiritual Self and lead to very different destinations.

New Skills and Awareness for a New Path

A new set of skills and awareness will be necessary for each individual seeking to home in on their Highest Path, whereby a sensory awareness is progressively opened up to enable an ongoing attunement to the sometimes invisible, and none too obvious, evolutionary trail. Subtle feelings of warmth and worthwhileness, a gentle curiosity, a perception of familiarity within a totally new pattern, an illumination of the creative faculty when aligning within the new field – all are valuable clues and pointers to a new direction, a new Path of discovery and involvement.

When such a Path is encountered by an individual, their subconscious mind will typically react from a mental/emotional level with all sorts of excuses as to why the new Path is "totally impossible to engage with" and, if one did, "a major failure will be experienced". And some of the following might be quite typical:

"I have no training for this kind of activity".

"If I changed occupations, it would take many months before I could generate sufficient income to live on".

"What do I know about (the new occupation)? I'm a (name of function within old occupation)".

"I would be letting down my existing employer/partners/co-workers/clients if I left now".

"I decided years ago that I was going to be a (name of function within old occupation) and I'm not changing now –I'm too old to change".

All the while, the Gateway to the new Path is open and waiting right in front of the individual's nose. Just beyond the Gateway, the new reality of the Path allows the new entrant to make a rapid start in the new Direction, with the required resources becoming available, often quite unexpectedly.

In this situation, when looked at objectively, it is the practice of the "old occupation" which is fraught with difficulty, because the individual has changed to such an extent that there is no longer a good alignment with that old line of work. Alternatively, the individual never had been aligned, and keeping up pretences has taken up more and more unproductive energy each year. The old motivations of high earnings, prestige, long holidays (or whatever), became less and less meaningful.

We are inclined to look at these situations of mismatch between individuals and their work as a particular example of the massive distortions which can occur when the exercise of free will has taken the individual out of alignment with the God force and Spirit. Within Western industrialised countries, the mainstream belief tends to be that an individual human is quite separate from the Spiritual Realities; for many there is no belief in Deity at all. In this separateness, the individual just goes ahead and makes decisions of all kinds within a mental, emotional, and physical structure directly connected to the selfish, ego-gratification orientated subconscious mind. Even among those on the Spiritual Path and those who have some "belief in God", the tendency is to make decisions at the subconscious level described above and then seek either support or forgiveness from God afterwards.

As the Divine Feminine and Divine Masculine balance becomes more fully present on Earth, as part of the evolution to Fifth Dimensional Consciousness, it is vitally important for every individual on the Spiritual Path (and those wishing to be) to understand as a basic working axiom that they are indeed an integral part of God and Spirit, truly seamlessly connected. With sustained commitment and focus, this working axiom can grow to the direct experience of Spirit, which is the field of access to God.

A Spiritual Basis for Decision Making

From this perspective of the reality of the individual's unity with God, a normal practice before any decision point (whether about work, business or other activity) is to consult with this Infinite Energy, of which we are all fully a part, to see how the Light Energy is flowing around the decision parameters. With clear perception, the whole need for a "decision" in a mainstream tradition fades away as the direction of the action required becomes quite clear, without the need for a traditional debate of "pros and cons". All that is needed is clear observation, connection to the Light through the Heart Centre, followed by relevant action. We call this "decision flow". The recognition within this Attunement of the individual being an integral part of God and Spirit, implies and requires that there is a natural Path to follow around each context of decision and choice – a Path which is Blessed and Illuminated.

We have chosen in this chapter to discourse on the relationship between an individual and God, and how this affects decision-making, because so many inappropriate decisions are being made in the career and workplace arena, day in and day out. Clearly these principles are of much broader application – in fact they can be applied to every facet of human existence, and we shall return to them in our last chapter about preparing for the Revolution of 2012 and beyond.

As individuals become more attuned with God through the field of Spirit, the new paradigm of "decision flow" changes the whole daily practice and experience of activity within their workplace. The impact is far beyond the actual identification and selection of a new Path of working endeavour, which is the vital first phase of realignment with God and Spirit.

Most work situations of the more responsible sort, particularly when one is working for one's own business or professional practice, require an ongoing stream of choices and decisions around every aspect of the enterprise with which the individual is engaged. Traditional decision-making is based on mental and physical learning, all kinds of past experience, and attempts to match or at least relate the past to fit the current situation. All this gives way to that State of Attunement in which we can perceive the "decision flow" in and around the apparent choices.

As an expression of the Unity within Spiritual Realms on Earth or in other dimensions, this Path contains within it all the elements of a situation which need to be considered. These include the Heart-felt aspirations of the various participants in the situation, as well as the relevant practical business parameters (like scheduling and resources available), which comprise the hands-on elements apparent to all closely concerned with the decision or choice – the exoteric facts of the business situation.

The "decision flow" Attunement allows all the elements outlined above to interact with each other and reach a stable equilibrium with a specific conclusion to act or not to act. If the conclusion is to act, then the direction and timing will be clearly indicated, and the resources needed will be either available or will be in the process of becoming available. On the other hand, if the conclusion is not to act, it will be clear whether the situation needs to be revisited for further review (and within what time span) or whether it's just a non-starter in the long run.

The participants in the "decision flow" situation will experience something between emotional uplift, relief, and a feeling of calm acceptance, depending on their depth of Attunement. Even those individuals, still primarily functioning on a mental level, will be enabled to feel some sensation broadly related to having a "gut feeling" with regard to the conclusion and outcome of the process.

This reflective, open, and insightful approach to reaching decisions is in striking contrast to the mental/rational/ego dominated process so prevalent in government, corporations, and many traditional organisations. A complex of physical, emotional, and mental factors jostle for position, and personal or departmental advantage. There is little regard for the higher aspects of the situation in terms of the real needs of the organisations' customers or other constituents, let alone of society as a whole. The decision process will be seen as just one more episode in an ongoing competition for power, self-aggrandisement, domination, and personal reward. It is little wonder that so many decisions by these types of institutions do not address the real and challenging business issues of the medium and long term. Instead, a bundle of short term trade-offs are agreed which satisfy the greed, lust for power, self-importance and other base motivations of the various participants.

The effect of the growing balancing presence of the Divine Feminine and the Fifth Dimensional Consciousness is to steadily disable this discordant way of operating. The motivation and drives of an individual continuing to embrace the old third dimensional ways of operating will mutate to such a degree of baseness that even the short-term tradeoffs become largely unattainable. The unconstrained lusts and greed increasingly drown out any former tendency to compromise, leading to major malfunction for the organisations involved.

Inspired Creativity

Looking more deeply now at the nature of business operations at the more refined levels of Attunement, we can observe that using the framework of "decision flow" greatly facilitates the identification and implementation of Divinely inspired choice. It can also be used positively and powerfully in the accessing of Spiritual creativity within the operation of the business or professional practice. All the business parameters and product/service integrity can be recognised as part of a framework of energy interactions. A Spiritually Attuned individual can address this framework in the context of whatever elements within the framework are deemed to require creative change or evolution, and then observe the "creativity flow" in and around these elements. This flow can reveal previously unnoticed connections between constituent elements, as well as bringing into focus new directions and qualities of outreach to customers and suppliers.

This does not have to be a complicated or difficult process, but it does require a substantial inner shift of orientation away from the old, traditional, rational, and sequential ways of solving "problems" by thinking "hard" about them. "Hard" is an appropriate term to use about attempting to change elements in a workplace situation and their inter-relationship, when the various human subconscious minds involved are firmly committed to continually recreating the past – the old and existing ways of operating.

To allow the "creativity flow" framework to become activated within organisations, the first and vital step is to release the inevitability of maintaining the old and existing procedures. Simultaneously, the belief in and commitment to the quality and integrity of the end product or service must at least be maintained and hopefully substantially improved, within the target range of pricing. The next step is to open the door to all possible input resources without any prior judgement about how they would finally be used in the new system.

The Spiritual Consciousness of "creativity flow" can be directly invited in by each individual participating in the redesign of procedures. Each participant in the process can reach some awareness of the new evolved patterns – while having, in all probability, a slightly different individual perspective on the shape and content of the pattern. Communicative and supportive teamwork will therefore continue to be a vital ingredient of the process. The great reward for the individual is finding these creative steps (or even leaps) within their understanding and practice of their particular occupation and experiencing the magic of the subtle contact with Spirit.

The courageous and inspired human resources development and job satisfaction consultants who have pioneered the opening of creative cooperation within the workplace during the last three decades have sowed many valuable seeds, some of which came to fruition. Within the massive uplift of consciousness brought about by the shift to Fifth Dimensional Consciousness, it will become a gentler climb to achieve the new alignment with creativity, compared with the steep mountainsides of times past. It will still need Faith to relax the mental and logical constraints of the old workplace and plunge into "creativity flow". However, with a much more supportive environment, an individual can take moderate steps of Faith, rather than having to make the proverbial leap that was demanded in the past.

As a significant proportion of businesses, professional practices, and other organisations convert to Spiritually-Attuned ways of operating, it will become more straightforward to find real solutions to the challenges facing human society. Individuals can choose to access Spiritual Inspiration as a regular input to their daily endeavours in the workplace. And a group of Enlightened and Attuned individuals meeting and working together can greatly multiply the sum of their separate individual achievements.

Fundamental changes of direction can open up and evolve appropriately in line with the needs of the true situation. The Spiritual Attunement will ensure that the new courses of action are both sound in themselves and relevant to the arenas they interact with, yet can maintain a flexibility as conditions may change. These practices will replace the largely ineffectual political trade-offs between departments and powerful individuals which, up to now, have all too often passed for solutions.

As more and more individuals develop the Spiritual Attunement in the workplace and practise both "decision flow" and "creativity flow", there will be a loosening of the ties linking an individual to a particular business, practice, or occupation. This will have the effect of creating much greater mobility in the way individuals can come together to work on a particular project and disperse afterwards, moving on to new horizons after the project's completion. This flexibility will also contribute to the solution of long standing "impossible" problems facing "life on Earth" and will facilitate a positive and safe path through 2012 and beyond.

CHAPTER TWELVE
The Move to Enlightened Self-Government

Within Western democracies, a consistent trend can be observed of governments and their instruments making more and more decisions for individuals, which in previous centuries used to be made by the individuals themselves. The justification for this takeover and control of personal life decisions is that government, and its various agencies, know better what an individual needs than that person does themselves.

Government has moved far beyond its historical role as the provider of law and order (including protection from foreign marauders) as well as being the arbiter between families and factions with conflicting interests. Currently, they seek to inflict compulsory medical treatment, standard school education for children, and very detailed safety standards for a multitude of different industries, as well as personal activities. They regularly intervene in commercial decisions in business and also with parental decisions within families.

The ongoing justification is that the business operators, parents, or whoever else attracts governments' unfavourable attention, are incapable of making the "right" decisions according to a collection of criteria currently in use in government circles. But these collections of criteria change and continue to change as political fads, fashions, and beliefs come and go.

Political parties often play a significant role in these over-centralised distortions, bringing forward old beliefs and past reactions to perceived problems as the ideological replacement for the real situation in the "here and now". Many of these interventions go far beyond any natural sense of maintaining law and order in an earthly sense, let alone according to Spiritual Principles and Laws.

Need for Karmic Opportunities

The fundamental Spiritual Principle is for each individual to choose their own course in life, which will broadly reflect the experiences they need to have for their evolutionary progress. Because of events and actions taken or not taken in other earthly existences, individuals will be energetically drawn to experience specific related situations in this life. This will enable them to have the opportunity to balance out some of those previous events and actions. They learn this balance by handling the situations positively, creatively, and without infringing on the rights of others to experience their own evolution.

Without freedom and the opportunity to make mistakes and learn from them, it is difficult for an individual to work constructively through their Karmic inheritance. Government and related authorities regularly attempt to eliminate opportunities for things in life to "go wrong", which means differently from how authorities believe things "should be". Hence there are fewer and fewer events and situations allowed to take place outside of a narrow path of "approved activities". This is one reason for more and more people experiencing their Karmic curriculum through personal illness and decay of the physical body, which perversely is regarded as normal by government authorities.

In the field of health and disease, government intervention has been singularly unsuccessful, other than for "law and order" aspects such as public hygiene and sanitation. Even in these fields, they have failed to prevent the massive chemical contamination of conventional food production with adverse run-off side effects for water supplies in agricultural areas.

Government Distortion of Health Systems

To be successful in achieving health as a "normal state of being" requires that education and wisdom be applied consistently at an individual level with regard to the true causes of health or its lack. The government-supported paradigm of using pharmaceutical drugs and surgery to try and eliminate symptoms of disease often results in the reappearance of the original symptoms and /or a new set of symptoms in another part of the body. Since the underlying causes remain unidentified and untreated, the state of imbalance and disease continues its course until such time that the causes are addressed, or the individual's body dies.

More and more governments have assumed the power to be the sole arbiter of what treatments shall be available and actually used. They even carry this to the extent of sometimes imprisoning highly capable practitioners of effective therapies, when the government authority chooses not to recognise the efficacy of those treatments.

To bolster this approach, people's financial resources are compulsorily sequestered through some form of taxation or insurance. This leaves little to be spent on freely chosen health practices, which effectively address the actual causes of health and disease.

In a more balanced world, without this extreme level of government intervention, an individual would have the choice to find the practitioner who could best address their needs within their own budget. Non-medical treatments would naturally gain a very large share of the healing market, because of their low cost and their effectiveness at addressing both causes and symptoms at Spiritual, emotional and physical levels.

The modest political profile of these alternative practitioners aligns with their primary focus on healing their clients effectively and thus building a strong practice. They do not need to have government authorities rigging their market to restrict competition from other providers of health and healing services in order for them to be successful and effective practitioners. They do need a level playing field of competition.

In marked contrast, the conventional medical services in Western industrial countries typically consume 10-15% of their countries' national income, yet are so ineffective at healing and curing their "patients" that the various doctors and hospitals stay in business mainly because of the massive tax revenues and /or insurance premiums reserved for their exclusive operation, maintenance, and upkeep.

With both revenue raising systems of tax revenues and insurance premiums, the receiver of medical services is not the person who pays the provider, thus obviating most customer feedback and choice. Because of the relatively low efficacy of many of their treatments, a preferential and semi-monopoly market position has been established to prevent them losing market share to more effective providers. The role of the pharmaceutical companies is self evident. They derive very large profits from this semi-monopoly situation and make substantial contributions to the re-election of the politicians, who create and continue to protect the favoured status of the medical services.

Government Distortion of Education Provision

Another field, in which government monopoly control distorts the availability of the broad variety of facilities needed by the end-user, is in education for children. In this realm also, massive tax revenues are diverted to the provision of a standard model of schooling to provide academic education, which happens to meet the needs of only a small number of the children. They do not address the actual individual needs of a child to learn in an appropriate environment and atmosphere.

Ignoring the need for supportive teacher attitudes and understanding of the learning process suitable for each child, the governmental authority in most systems lays down that children should fit into the standard model of schooling. And if they don't, they are "misfits", "lacking intelligence and concentration", and/or are "just plain lazy".

If parents should want to make a separate provision of an educational programme, which fits the child's needs more appropriately, they have to pay twice: once for the unwanted standard school, then again for the actual programme selected for the individual child. It is little wonder that the evolution and provision of alternative and evolving patterns of education, to suit the current times, are so stilted and restricted by the artificially created shortage of revenue, except in a few enlightened locations, where provision of school vouchers have begun to enable a more level playing field.

Choice Restricted by Government Control

So in both these fields of health and education, the government authorities have set up their most favoured semi-monopolies, which substantially deny or restrict individuals in making appropriate choices, which would otherwise suit their own and their families' needs. We have singled out the health and education fields as prime examples of the distortions resulting from governments taking over choices and decision making which belong rightly to individuals and families.

The long arm of government also reaches out to control, or attempt to control, most arenas of human life: the workplace and the labour force, retirement systems, consumer protection, environmental protection, and many interventions in the commercial and business fields. With the move to the Fifth Dimensional Reality and the return of the Divine Feminine, fundamental issues which need to be urgently addressed are: to what extent (if at all) are governments actually wiser than individuals and their representative associations; and how does government need to change as some individuals become more enlightened and hence innately more self-sufficient?

Wisdom and Integrity in Decision-Making Hierarchy

It is a universal law of Spirit that any Hierarchy achieves that role through a concentration of Love, Light, Purity and Wisdom. Selfless service is the norm and ensures that choices and decisions are for the greater and highest good. On the basis of this comparison, most politicians and government officials need to resume more basic functions in human society.

Modern Western governments have access to a vast range of information from a multitude of sources, but their ability to use this information wisely is constrained by the modest level of understanding with which it is focused by the politicians and civil service officials. Instead, the combination of political realism, competitive ruthlessness in the personal pursuit of power, and the normal practice of making trade-offs between Truth and political expediency are the principal ingredients which take political officials (both elected and unelected) to the top positions of power and influence.

Unfortunately the traits and attitudes, which take them in this way to the upper levels of government, are far from those required for balanced, in-depth insight into the wide variety of issues being addressed by government. They are also quite separate from the characteristics of Higher Spiritual Consciousness, which would enable decisions made by government to be for the best interests of all people involved in the long-term interest of Humanity.

The Higher Spiritual Consciousness would ensure that the interests of the Earth in general, and Nature in particular, are fully taken into account in the development of policy and associated decisions. While an occasional official in the present system may develop some Spiritual Wisdom in their later years, the political and bureaucratic culture from whence they came continues to severely constrain their scope to introduce Higher Wisdom into any decision making process.

As the Fifth Dimensional Consciousness increasingly pervades the Earth during the run up to 2012, the engrained patterns of tradition and the blocking effect of the group consciousness will make central government one of the last holdouts of "politics as usual". This increases the urgency for political power, currently concentrated at the centre, to be substantially passed back to local community and individual levels, since the latter can respond much more readily to the new energy environment and are more open to putting inspirational decision making into practice.

Self-Governing Communities

The starting point for change is for each individual to take responsibility for their own life, using their own Spiritual Heart-Centre as the connection with unlimited Wisdom and Power to provide total support for this crucial step. As they develop greater inner strength and insight, they can link up with people of similar orientation to form groups which can validate their alternative experience of life on an ongoing basis. In this way, new communities can come together defined by insight and Spiritual sensibility on the one hand, and the strength of discipline and Right Action on the other, rather than just because folks happen to live in the same geographical area.

As these new communities learn to concentrate their energies and focus on each situation they deal with by attuning with Spiritual Truth, they will develop quite disproportionate power and influence because of that focus. The beliefs and projections of a traditional secular group come predominantly from a common ground of individual subconscious memories, combined with reactions to those memories and current situations. In contrast, the Spiritually attuned group and communities can create their own manifestations powerfully by together focusing on the inspired Higher vibrational energies now available.

In the new Fifth Dimensional environment, when a whole group clearly visualises, feels, and projects a new Reality coming into existence, then the desired outcome will come into being aligned with the high Spiritual values involved or affected, regardless of lack of support or even opposition from established groups or institutions, which do not have the alignment with Spirit.

Contained within this contrast of approaches are the rudiments of a major transfer of power from the old order of centralised, bureaucratic government to the real New Order of self-empowered, Spiritually-Attuned individuals and groups, who have left behind the ego driven self-gratification self to address the True fullness of life on Earth. This will go beyond just human needs, and far beyond the demands of some favoured minority, in the old tradition of corrupt centralised government.

The Passing of the Old Order

It is not expected that the operators and beneficiaries of the old system will cede their power and influence with alacrity. It is more likely that their established and practical methods of wielding and maintaining power will begin to lose their effectiveness; somehow information that they wish to remain secret will become widely known, and the true motives for policies and related decisions will become public knowledge.

Their hold on power will become slippery; they find that there is nothing to grip, nothing certain to move forwards with, nothing to push against. Without reliability and predictability, the old skills of holding onto power diminish into ineffectiveness as issues come up requiring decision which have no precedent and can only be addressed and solved by alignment with the

Light and with genuine caring, insight, and benevolent understanding of a greater Whole.

The old arrogance of power, stemming from the belief that the government knew better what to do in any situation than those they were ruling, collecting money from, or otherwise harassing as rivals, is in the process of being replaced by enlightened individuals practising self-government. This is happening both individually, in community, and in functional groups. Alignment with Truth and an ongoing wish to individually and collectively follow the Path of Highest Evolution, replace the indulgence of lust for power and ego self-gratification. And within the harmony of that Path are the varied individual choices which have a built-in compatibility with each other.

This may seem a radical agenda for a world that has known little else than varying degrees of blind authoritarian government for most of two millennia, but it is the direction of change that is happening anyway. So it is suggested that the wisest course is to prepare for the new state of Enlightened self-government by going within to attune to Spirit on a regular basis.

It is important to seek harmony and loving balance in all interactions with others, and seek solutions which encompass the interests and needs of all parties involved in and around an issue, and of all constituencies affected. The recommendations in the chapter on the opening of the Heart-Centre are directly relevant to these evolved processes. If in doubt, ask Spirit for help in Attuning and establishing an appropriate direction.

A prime understanding about achieving harmonious Spiritual Order and cooperation within and between communities, and in replacement of authority-driven government, is that there is a Spiritual Design for the evolution of human society – a clear framework with which to align. As individuals tune in to this Design they will perceive enough of the overall energy pattern, despite its complexity, to make sense of their own and their community's situations, as well as an enlarged perspective on their particular role and participation in the Design.

But the crucial difference is that, with this process of many people Attuning to the Spiritual Design for human society and for the Earth's evolution, their perceptions will be mutually consistent, while maintaining their personal perspective on their individual roles. This enables a community of Attuned individuals to consistently find agreement when they get together to discuss an issue. They can avoid getting into the rancorous kind of disagreement, which happens all too frequently under the old systems of authoritarian and adversarial government, with all its competing and self-focused political factions.

In the new paradigm of cooperative endeavour, balance and harmony will automatically be created through implementation of the Spiritual Design coming from the concentrated Wisdom of the Hierarchy, every constituency's needs are addressed fully, Nature will be sustained and respected without contamination or pollution, yet the needs of the human population will also be satisfied.

The Spiritually Attuned individuals within an Attuned community will be able to make significant decisions at this local level because of their alignment to the Spiritual design, in all its perfection and its infinite ability to come up with balanced solutions to every challenge. This taking of responsibility on a continual basis, through Attunement to all aspects, will ensure the wellbeing of the community and the flourishing of all the realms of Nature. Solutions will manifest for the needs of individual lives, the needs of their local community, and the needs of the wide ranging "community of communities" throughout the world.

Nationality and cultural patterns will become part of a gentle expression of Life and its content, something to be shared with others, rather than some magnet of habitual allegiance, competitive motivation, and constant repetition of old thought and behaviour pattern.

The concept of a national government imposing its will through centrally conceived plans and decisions on a specific community, or groups of communities, is crumbling, as people realise more and more that national governments have more allegiance to their own operators, paymasters and fundraisers, other large institutions, other national governments, and even international organisations, than to the general population of the country they claim to represent.

A Critical Mass of Enlightenment

The move to Enlightened self-government is one of the most visible changes stemming from the manifestation of Fifth Dimensional Consciousness and Reality on Earth. It requires that enough individuals connect directly with their Higher Spiritual Self, as described in previous chapters, as the source of their daily life experience. This is in sharp contrast to the old pattern of being primarily directed by their subconscious mind endeavouring, as always, to recreate the past and feed the ego self-gratification self.

With enough individuals focused on this Higher Consciousness of Truth, a critical mass of Enlightenment and connection can prevail, even though they interact on a daily basis with many individuals still functioning in a subconscious driven third dimensional reality.

As the Cosmic Energy environment raises its frequency to higher and higher octaves, there is an infinite reservoir of strength and support available to be used at the Fifth Dimensional level of Consciousness by those who align with it. In contrast, there is less and less supportive energy at the third dimensional level.

Thus profound and wide-ranging changes in Consciousness can happen now and throughout the run up to 2012 and beyond, which might otherwise have taken millennia to come about. Without this revolutionary shift of Consciousness, only small incremental changes in society and government systems would be feasible. These changes, by their very incremental nature, are still using the existing distorting foundations from times past and, however well intended, will perpetuate those distortions.

With the shift to the Fifth Dimensional Reality and the re-emergence of the Divine Feminine in excellent balance with the Divine Masculine, a true revolution and enlightened self government is, at last, under way.

CHAPTER THIRTEEN
Education as a Life Experience

Prior to the industrial age, most adults worked in around or close to their home, very often engaged directly in the production and preservation of food. This work might have related to raising crops, breeding and tending animals and birds, fishing or hunting. Often a whole household would undertake the operation of a farm, however small, and the children would be taking on small tasks from an early age. For them, life was about what they witnessed, and gradually participated in, more and more each day – learning and practising the work skills being exercised all around them by parents and other adults.

In a community that supported itself by hunting or fishing, the accumulation of skills by children would be similar, but with a clear threshold to be passed through when they were taking on their first hunting expedition away from the home/community base. In the small minority of households supported by a skilled trade or service, the father would sometimes spend time working away from home, involved in production or service at a distant location, like building a cathedral, other contract work or even fighting a war. In this scenario, the son(s) would receive more intermittent training in the father's skill, until they were old enough to travel with him.

Despite the large numbers of variations within the above themes in a multitude of societies, there is a consistent pattern of children learning by watching and helping their parents and/or other adults performing their daily work functions. Within the daily processes, accumulated understandings were passed along for generations, being gradually and easily absorbed and integrated by the children living and working alongside the adults. Changes in these patterns would evolve organically out of necessity, inspiration, and creativity.

Contemporary Separation

The contrast with the upbringing and training of children in contemporary industrialised countries is extreme. The separation of children from adults, who often work outside the home, stretches from birth through adolescence. For many families, one or both parents work outside the home on a full or part time basis and the only direct experience of "work" by children is limited to domestic chores. Their learning about work or business activities outside the home is firmly linked to the emotions (positive or negative) about these activities expressed by parents or other adults, sometimes augmented by a story or two.

Apart from some involvement with tasks related to household functioning, most children come to equate "work" with the somewhat dry diet of academic learning, in which they are required to engage for some ten to eighteen years. With a curriculum largely devoid of emotional or Spiritual content, children are conditioned to process concepts mentally in response to instructions from an authority figure, regardless of any feeling of connection or interest in the material being offered.

After years of such exposure, adolescents leaving school or college to begin their careers, have little connection with their deeper inner aptitudes and ways of fulfilment, let alone their higher Spiritual Destinies, those Inner Paths awaiting Illumination and activation. The stories of mid-career crisis often relate to the eventual emergence of an individual's inner truths about what they like to do, and what they themselves really feel about being personally creative in life. For it is these glimmerings of Light which show the way into the Highest Spiritual Path for an individual. This is a Path through which they can feel that sense of Oneness with the Divine, and through which they can work and interact with their Inner Self at the deepest level.

New Approaches to Life Education

Earlier, we described the natural development of a child learning from the adults around them. We have also referred earlier to the very individual nature of children's needs for educational experiences – often quite different needs from the standard school model providing academic education. In this chapter we are going to look in greater detail at education as an integral ongoing aspect of life experience, beginning at birth and continuing without a break until the "death" transition.

In early childhood, there is a great need for the child to be in the continual presence of a Heart-Centred parent or other adult, who is attuned continuously to the needs of the child, way beyond providing care by rote or from a checklist. Breast feeding for at least the first three years is vital for the full development of the child's immune system and other physical organs. Any food or drink must be totally free of sugar, salt and chemical additives, to allow full development of intuitive perception and awareness.

Harmonious sound, light, and aromas are of great importance, along with the use (to the greatest extent possible) of natural fabrics and play materials, rather than synthetics. Research has shown that a young child exposed to Mozart has significantly faster cognitive development than one who is not. This is just the tip of the iceberg in the identification of the evolutionary effects of sound vibration, but a welcome one indeed.

To enable young children to develop naturally within the Fifth Dimensional Consciousness into which they are being born (or are graduating into), a consciously created environment needs to be established of programmes of sound, backed up by related programmes of light and aromas of compatible and mutually resonating wavelengths, individually attuned to the evolutionary needs of each child.

The discordant sounds of television, rock music, most Hollywood movies, two-stroke engines, road drills, and similar, should be absent during the first crucial years of life. It is in this stage that sensitive foundations are being laid for the Highest Evolution and harmonious integration of the physical, mental, emotional and etheric bodies.

To facilitate the creation of these ideally suitable environments, families and interested individuals within communities will need to cooperate and pull resources for the creation of such facilities. Perhaps part of the energy and enthusiasm which currently goes into gardening, sports, and hobbies can be applied to the development of sound, light, and aroma "immersion" environments. The technology, understandings and facilities can also be used for adults' heightened evolutionary development, as well as for deep relaxation and joyful inner exploration.

By using these sound, light, and aroma experimental facilities, the young children will learn and be able to learn continuously throughout life with great ease, and there will be no need to stipulate a particular age to start schooling. Rather, children will begin to sample various kinds of learning facilities in their own time. They will start with modest exposures, while they develop a sense of what kinds of learning opportunities appeal most to their creative and evolving Spirit.

As they follow their own path of exploration and experience, some children need intense, creative physical exercise as a major part of their experiential content. Others need creative art, music, craftwork, creative writing, and/ or theatrical work as the major thrust of their studies. Another type of approach would focus on all the physical skills, including science and engineering, that are needed in the adult world in an old apprenticeship tradition of children learning to do all the activities they see their parents and other adults involved with, and using these as the link and understanding to their theoretical background knowledge and understanding.

All these approaches to education and learning are far removed from today's academic schools (whether government or privately founded), which do indeed suit a minority of the child population. Currently, only the Waldorf system, some individual private schools, and home education begin to address the needs for a wide variety of non-academic approaches. Overall, an important feature of this enlightened approach will be a reduction of academic teaching for children. There would be more emphasis in favour of physical exercise and physiological development, creative art and music, craftwork, creative theatrical activities, and a broad range of participation in "real life" adult activities, in line with ancient traditions described at the beginning of this chapter.

A crucial feature of the Fifth Dimensional learning facilities is the ease of access to and transfer between alternative environments. This will enable children to experience a particular mix of educational approaches, that is appropriate for the individual child, in the sequence and time span each of them needs. This is a substantial departure from the patterns of narrow but in-depth training provided by academic schools and requires a major change in the framework of understanding of what children need to experience as they evolve and grow up.

The fundamental truth, within the Fifth Dimensional paradigm of education, is that an individual child will instinctively be drawn to the learning and experiences they need. This is a similar pattern for a child raised on fresh organic food (without sugar, salt and gluten), who will instinctively be drawn each day to the selection of foods that they need for their individual nutrition and balance.

For this mobility between different places of learning to be an everyday reality for each child, the framework of daily living needs to have flexibility beyond current concepts of family organisation and scheduling. How can an individual child have a daily freedom of choice related to how they feel on waking each morning, without an obligation to follow the preferences of the day before? It requires community trust, engagement and cooperation between families to facilitate this level of unencumbered freedom of choice for every child. Parents may choose to facilitate a particular avenue of learning and experimental activities, while children can choose their activity, without any constraint arising from where their own parent will be operating that day.

There will obviously be a substantial role for full-time professionals providing skilled and expert "experiences" in many arenas. A key difference from traditional arrangements, however, would be that each of these facilitators would live in the community they serve and would be surrogate parents, not just teachers within a narrow subject corridor.

Education an Integral Part of Life Evolution

The themes of participation and individual experience encapsulate the scope of education in the new times. Rather than being something mainly for children, education will be seen as an integral part of an individual's evolution throughout each incarnation in physical form. There will be a continual focus on drawing out the unlimited inner essence of each individual with ever increasing breadth and depth.

The source of the curriculum for each individual will be by Spiritual Inspiration coming through multiple sources with consistent purity of content. There will be an important role for Spiritually-Attuned guides and counsellors who can home in on the Path of Highest Evolution by direct observation and perception.

Wave Communication for Accessing Knowledge

A great benefit of the expanded consciousness at Fifth Dimensional wavelengths will be a gradual phasing out of languages, as we know them, in favour of wave communication between individuals. This process is like a broadband version of psychic connection will also be fundamentally important for storing and accessing many forms of knowledge.

A substantial part of adult education will be advanced training in wave communication and using it to access the technology and wisdom of other Fifth Dimensional Consciousness civilisations and, at the right time, individual instructors from such civilisations. This training will also enable the adults to keep up with the new generations of children who are born with great facility in wave communication, and many of whom may never develop a high skill level in word languages. And the efficiency of wave communication is far beyond that of our current word languages.

Far higher levels of understanding, insight, and comprehension will be attained from just a few hours of focused engagement each week, than from full-time education in the current modes. This will leave the remainder of the week for a wide variety of working and artistic activities for adults, and for the creative and physical development activities for children (and all ages) mentioned previously.

To complement the vast mind expansion enabled by wave communication, physical development for all ages will include the kind of movement, stretching and balance routine within yoga, chi-gong, tai-chi and eurhythmy, and will be available from the earliest years of a child's life right through to the last years of a greatly extended lifetime. It will also enable the Heart Centre to grow and function within an integrated network of Mind, Body and Spirit – truly a holistic living experience.

There is already a precursor of recorded wave communication in the form of a silent healing recording produced by World Development Systems Ltd in the UK. This broadcasts "silently" the wavelengths of homeopathic formulas and flower remedies (outside wavelengths which are audible for humans), enabling the recipients to absorb whatever corrected patterns they need through a sympathetic resonance.

This approach can even now be greatly expanded and applied to the sharing and absorption of most forms of knowledge and understanding. With the addition of audible sound and accompanying light patterns, the transfer of deep, balanced knowledge and understanding can become an everyday practice, continually tailored to an individual's needs and abilities through the self-selection of mutual resonance.

The combination of the wave communication development with the sound, light, and physical experiential learning will empower the functioning of human consciousness at the highest levels of creation and activity throughout a greatly extended lifespan. Higher Attunement and achievement will be continually facilitated by selected wave communication aligned with supporting sound and light.

CHAPTER FOURTEEN
The Revolution of 2012 and Beyond

The Winter Solstice of 2012 will be a watershed in the evolution of the Earth and Humanity. In the six years up to that point in time, human experience on the Earthplane will be startling in its apparent ups and downs, as sometimes gut-wrenching changes take place, often without specific advance notice or expectation.

Some of these will be extraordinary land changes precipitated by earthquakes and volcanoes releasing built-up pressures, while water levels rise steadily as the polar ice melts. Both these patterns are inevitable as the North Pole moves inexorably towards its new location in the Himalayas.

As a concomitant to the vast reorganisation of humanity's ways of living outlined in earlier chapters, the location of the land and the climate appertaining will undergo a similar scale of near cataclysmic change. These land and climate rearrangements are equally important parts of the creation of a new Fifth Dimensional Consciousness on Earth. The vast expansion in Heart Consciousness, together with the effect of the balance of Spiritual Feminine/ Masculine Attunement, will provide the opportunity for individuals and communities to choose to be part of the new Fifth Dimensional Consciousness.

The energy and the ambience of the rearranged land will require humans of an elevated consciousness to live harmoniously in close juxtaposition and alignment with Nature. With this in mind, it is important for each individual on the Spiritual Path to cultivate a close connection and rapport with Nature in all her manifestations.

Relating to Nature will be of particular importance during these six years of dramatic and sometimes turbulent change up to 2012, and during the more Illuminated evolutionary period subsequent to that watershed Winter Solstice. In the period prior to that turning point, the ability to maintain that harmonious feeling of participation with Nature may well be the passport to finding oneself in the "right place at the right time" to maintain viable living conditions in daily life, while other areas undergo rearrangements of land masses and great bodies of water. That same ability enables an individual to cultivate land constructively and effectively for vital food supplies. It will also facilitate wise choices of land co-development as physical conditions stabilise in the years following 2012.

No doubt some people will reflect during these latter phases how much greater balance could have been achieved in their lives, and in their former communities, if they had developed this awareness and these skills before they became so critically essential for the maintenance of human life on Earth. They might even reflect further that if a significant number of community groups had developed and practised this consciousness in prior decades, how the patterns of evolution of land and water might have been more tranquil under the influence of this collective stewardship. Such regrets, coupled with aspiration for better options in hindsight, are quite normal under third dimensional consciousness, but they will phase out with the higher level of consciousness as we move forwards.

As time continues to speed up, people will experience the present and the future as being much closer together, if not actually happening simultaneously. This will naturally result in both time periods being treated with equal importance in decision-making frameworks. There will be no more of the "quick fix" mentality so beholden of third dimensional politicians, civil servants, and all too many company directors and managers.

Attunement to All Species on Earth

The replacement Consciousness of Fifth Dimensional "decision-flow" will require and innately incorporate the consideration of a multilateral range of issues and concerns, treating present and future situations with equal weight. The process will also fully include the welfare and needs of all natural species and the flow of energy within the elemental kingdoms of Fire, Water, Air, and Earth. The new approach will go far beyond the simple Win-Win concept of benign decision-making of third dimensional consciousness, which only addresses the needs and/or demands of human protagonists or competitors, for control of the same resources.

The new process will require Attunement to the needs and evolution of all participants in the process of living on Earth. And this in-depth consideration of these multiple universes within universes will not be conditional on the loudness or volume of communication from each micro-universe, but will rotate around a clearly communicated Spiritual Design providing for a balanced juxtaposition of species and their interacting habitats.

For example, it will be the prime focus and responsibility of those facilitating any decision involving land use, to attune to the needs expressed by the Nature Devas, and find harmonious solutions without detriment to the Divine Plan being unveiled. The procedure passed on from the North American Indians for several millennia of asking permission from the Devas before taking actions affecting a natural species, is directly relevant and an excellent precedent. Equally important is the complementary practice of giving thanks after a contribution by any natural species to human wellbeing and nourishment.

Adverse Physical Influences

In contemporary discussion of the phenomena of Global Warming, a variety of causes have been identified for the increase in sea water temperatures. The seemingly ever increasing CO_2 and other detrimental emissions into the atmosphere from industrial installations and motor vehicle exhausts have been recognised as being a significant contributor to Global Warming, by most individuals with some understanding of atmospheric weather patterns and ocean currents. They have recognised both the statistical correlation over time and the scientific perceptions of the creation of "greenhouse" conditions in the atmosphere along with major changes in ocean currents.

A few very perceptive observers have homed in on the contribution to Global Warming made by the weather and earthquake control technologies practised by the United States and Russia. Each time these technologies are used in intervention, the Earth's natural checks and balances are, in varying degrees, blocked or distorted. This leads to enormous pressures building up in key locations which will be released unpredictably by the Earth to achieve equilibrium.

Shifting of the Poles

Although there are various clues already apparent that the poles of the Earth are shifting, there is no obvious scientific cause for this extraordinary and dramatic change, nor any comprehensive data which illustrates its direction and progress. However, this is a phenomenon that is taking place because it is part of the Spiritual Design for the new form of the Earth at Fifth Dimensional Consciousness, rather than simply being a direct and inevitable consequence of current global imbalances.

There are various other directions and final layouts which could have been brought into being, but the North Pole moving to a new position in the Himalayas is part of the solution chosen by the Spiritual Hierarchy who are overseeing this vast transformation. It is an important part of a multi-dimensional Design.

The melting of the polar ice-caps and other frozen land masses has already been recorded as proceeding much faster than would be expected just from the rise in temperature. Special frequencies transmitted from the Sun have had a significant effect on speeding up the process of melting the ice. This will result in a rise in the sea level of twenty feet or more, making it difficult for existing coastal cities to remain viable.

Even the outstanding creative talents of Dutch engineers in constructing watertight sea defences around land which is below sea level, will be stretched to implement much beyond a few stop-gap solutions. The reduction of the importance of major coastal cities is part of a decision by the Spiritual Realms to have most of the surviving population residing and working in rural and semi-rural locations, where most resources needed for human existence can be produced naturally close to home.

Participating in the Spiritual Design

It is important to move beyond a "helpless victim" state of mind, when considering the major consequences of the physical rearrangements. It does not have to be a scenario where one is just responding to what appear to be adverse random events or rapidly changing situations, in which previous land utilisation is no longer possible.

A much more viable approach to the situation is to engage with the Spiritual Design, which lovingly provides for many safe havens for Humanity during the course of the sometimes intense landscape and seascape alterations. The "decision flow" approach, described in chapter eleven, is directly applicable to this process of finding the best safe location.

Rather than responding to the radical change in prospects with rejection, denial, anger, despair or similarly unfocused states, the reader is invited to consciously consider what is being positively offered. Choosing to join up with one of a variety of alternative groups and communities that are currently focused on creating long-term solutions, can enable a reasonably harmonious step along the path to Fifth Dimensional Consciousness living.

These groups have the intention to create viable Paths, which are a clear alternative to current and existing "modern civilisation". They are in no way intended to challenge or confront the old ways but to specifically provide a vehicle to ride the wave of change, both figuratively and sometimes, perhaps, literally.

Establishing Self-Sufficient Communities

Part of the Spiritual Vision and programme for the development of Fifth Dimensional Consciousness on Earth is to establish self-sufficient communities on each major existing land mass. The community locations within each land mass are being chosen in terms of land stability, a climate which will support human life, both during the run-up to 2012 and beyond. Many will be in places which have not been significantly affected or damaged by industrialised agriculture.

The communities' fundamental modus operandi will be to develop and demonstrate, on the most practical level, the value, feasibility and year-on-year viability of a Love-based Spiritual Reality being expressed consistently through continuous Heart Consciousness by each member of the community. New levels and patterns of Spiritual energy will be made available to each of these undertakings to enable the training for and practice of inner and outer Attunement. This will be the foundation of all activities and, indeed, their creative Inspiration. The members of the communities will be drawn together at a Heart level by a deep alignment and affinity with a shared Spiritual Reality.

The Spiritual Reality will be expressed, not only through creative working practices and achievements, but also through sacred dance, music and art. Health and healing will be maintained at a high level through a wide range of alternative therapies linked to individual and group practices, which build strength and alignment in the human body. For more insights into the approaches to be adopted by these communities, please see the appendix following this chapter.

There are plenty of other preparations that individuals and families can commence right away whatever their current location. They can find likeminded people within their own location and/or broader communities and look to set up together some group cooperative projects.

As external conditions become more challenging, people will become much more open to exploring new approaches to working with neighbours and friends on practical shared projects. These could include: joint cultivation of a large kitchen garden for food production, sharing and exchanging health treatments, group meditation, sacred dance and music, and so on.

As food supplies become less reliable, some city dwellers may feel motivated to move to more rural areas with their group. This will facilitate the development of a large enough productive garden to provide food directly all the year round for their families, and with some to spare.

Positive cooperation within a community can be stimulated and encouraged in times of doubt and adversity by the sense of shared needs being fulfilled. Going deeper into harmonious and constructive group relationship covering every aspect of life, always requires a major opening of the Heart Centre to allow Love energy to flow and connect on a normal and continuing basis. The sense of common purpose, acceptance of each other, the uplift experience through the generosity of giving, are only achieved through that Heart Opening and connection which we have described earlier.

Only through the Heart can alignment be reached with the Divine or Cosmic Law and principles, and Fifth Dimensional Consciousness manifested on Earth. This is why it is vital that Heart opening activities like Sufi zikr, Dances of Universal Peace, and yoga be practiced consistently, along with regular participation in drama and inspirational music, to establish these powerful and refined connections within.

A New Golden Age

In the early stages, life in these new forms of community may well be very demanding, but has been very true historically for the pioneers of most radically new endeavours, stretching back thousands of years. As knowledge of advanced techniques of cultivation, power generation, and building design become readily available, it will enable steady forward movement of the self-sufficient community concept and progressive levels of planning and implementation. Mutual guidance, assistance, and experience-sharing will save any community from getting blocked by a particular obstacle or challenge.

Over the centuries, many people on their individual Spiritual paths have yearned for a Golden Age when their dreams of a well-functioning, harmonious and mutually loving world would truly be continually present. For so long it has seemed that it would always remain in the abstract.

Now, in this extraordinary period of the run-up to 2012 and beyond, the promise of fundamental change is coalescing at last. The challenge for each individual is to find their way forward to being part of the New World at the highest possible vibration, and actually participate in that continuous joy and harmony dreamed after for so long. The Fifth Dimensional Consciousness, to which the Earth is ascending, offers each person the opportunity to realise limitless perfection, within their joyful participation in human life expressed at its most refined, truly a State of Grace.

FURTHER RESOURCES

Preparing for the Revolution of 2012 is an enormous ongoing project. We recommend follow-up reading to broaden understanding of what is happening during the years prior to 2012 and the prospects for the New Age to follow.

BOOKS & WEBSITES:

Our website: www.revolutionof2012.net

"The Sanctus Germanus Prophecies" by Michael P. Mau PhD
from The Sanctus Germanus Foundation at:
www.sanctusgermanus.net

"The Red Letters" by Master KH
from The DK Foundation at:
www.dkfoundation.co.uk

"Cancer: – Why We're Still Dying to Know the Truth"
By Phillip Day
Credence Publications
PO Box 3, Tonbridge, TN12 9ZY UK
www.credence.org

World Development Systems Ltd at:
www.wds-global.com

Dr. Julian Whittaker, MD at:
www.drwhitaker.com

Dr. David Williams, MD at:
www.drdavidwilliams.com

APPENDIX

PROPOSAL TO ESTABLISH SELF-SUFFICIENT COMMUNITIES

Introduction

There is a growing realization that human life and its various endeavours need to change significantly in the next few years from the patterns explicit during the nineteenth and twentieth centuries. The ways of industrialisation, urbanisation, and destructive approaches to food procurement are creating instability and non-sustainability in human interaction with the land. The huge cocktail of chemicals created by this industrial age permeates all of our air, water, and food.

Atmospheric pollution has led to multiple distortions in Earth's ecosystems leading to adverse weather conditions, crop failures, the creation of (more) desert-like terrain, the deterioration and demise of birds, sea creatures, and animals in the wild, as their habitat has been damaged or destroyed. Lands and water have been poisoned by toxic materials, with dire consequences for humans, animals, birds, insects, and other life forms.

Global warming is destabilising climates and directly upsetting the eco-systems that plants, sea creatures, animals and humans live in. Humanity can truly be said to have forgotten the Oneness of all creation and expresses the ultimate blindness in the killing of its own environment and life-support systems.

The partial response of governments and of the mainstream of humanity has been to establish new protocols for atmospheric emissions, protection of fish, birds, and other decimated species.

All too often, the follow-through has been intermittent or half-hearted, instead of the revolutionary change of course which is desperately needed, if mankind is to continue on the Earth.

A few minor successes in some arenas have been overwhelmed, in aggregate, by ongoing blatant disregard of the Earth's needs and the "requirements" of contemporary living by unconscious societies, throughout the many parts of the world. The end result is that mainstream approaches to land use, building design and construction, energy use and power supply, as well as health maintenance and development, are not viable and consistent with the current and increasing levels of population, even without the huge shifts to industrialisation taking place in vast countries which were predominantly rural until just a few years ago. There is a great need for mankind to re-establish a respectful and loving Spiritual connection to Nature. It is vitally important that we create a new paradigm in agriculture based on sound knowledge and practices.

The Elders of the Hopis and other American Indian tribes have gently communicated that Humanity is about to make the transition from the current patterns of existence to a radically different way of living. This change is so profound that they regard it as a passage to a new world.

The Elders recall a recurring evolutionary pattern of Humanity's undergoing a slow gradual rise from simple communities living in harmony with Nature to a period of technologically advanced societies with widely shared cultural values emanating from a dominant power (Atlantis, USA etc.). Each time this "advanced level" is reached, the destructive imbalances spiral out of Human control and the world crashes back to a primitive level once more, so that the prime lesson of Oneness and its inherent respect for the evolution of all living beings can be relearned and relived.

Similar understandings are available from the records of past civilisations (the biblical Noah's Ark, Plato's and ancient Egyptian's descriptions of Atlantis etc.) but the American Indians' understandings are of special importance because of their unbroken lineage of direct oral history being passed on from generation to generation.

Implicit within the wisdom from these ancient sources are the activities of small groups of people who, during the latter part of the evolutionary pattern, endeavour to maintain balance within their Human existences by maintaining a high level of harmony with Nature and avoiding the polluting lifestyles of the mass consciousness. In this way, the old and true knowledge of holistic life on Earth is sustained and carried forward to the new world.

Recently, it has been communicated from high Spiritual Realms that the evolution of the Earth, in these early years of the 21st Century, will lead to a very different kind of "New World". Far from crashing down to a primitive level of physical living, the plan is for the Earth to rise to a Fifth Dimensional Consciousness, even while going through its quite dramatic physical transformations. This means that very advanced Spiritual understandings and technology will be subtly introduced to enable humans to coexist with in harmony with Nature, while living with simple refinement. The challenge for individual humans is to stay with the Earth as she evolves to these higher vibrations.

Although no part of the Earth is immune from the environmental disasters taking place elsewhere, Spiritual Guidance has indicated that it is possible, with clear intent, to establish separate enclaves to begin the process of re-Attunement with natural processes. These enclaves, in harmony with Nature, can enable life to be sustained, not withstanding major degradation in mainstream living conditions.

Against the background of deteriorating conditions on Earth, the establishment of balanced residential communities as relative oases of harmony offer many benefits. Besides enabling the stability of reliable food and energy supplies, a major educational role would be addressed by creating a showcase for a new era of human life. By demonstration and outreach, current and evolving methodologies for food production, abundant energy, and effective healing can be made available for a larger attuned community in multiple locations, on several continents.

Space would also be created for the expression of varied forms of sacred dance, music and meditative prayer. Therefore, an underlying inspiration is the Spiritual and personal development of the individuals resident in the community, of visitors, and those in the outside world who are attuning to similar wavelengths of Fifth Dimensional Consciousness.

The proposal here is quite specific and is a response to the more general matters discussed above. Establishing largely self-sufficient communities is to help the Earth maintain balance, as well as help ourselves and those who are drawn to these enclaves of Light and Consciousness. This is of clear value on all levels and represents a grounded and reasonable response to the issues humankind faces at this juncture in its evolution.

The Design of a New Community

It is both important and interesting to examine each facet of living physically on the land in terms of identifying what combinations of resources would deliver a high quality of life experience simultaneously with creating a positive interaction with Nature and the elementals.

To live on land, which is positively energised at all times would provide an uplifting experience for all those thus exposed. The techniques of biodynamic farming are well proven for producing large quantities of highly nutritional food which can enable the achievement of self-sufficiency in vegetables and grains. The practice of Agnihotra has demonstrated the immense increase of agricultural productivity (in terms of both quality and quantity) available from this focused application of dedicated love and nurturing for lands of many different hues.

Creative building designers have shown us a myriad of approaches to manifesting good-looking buildings, which are also spacious, light, easy to maintain, yet consume little or no energy. Such energy as may be required is attained (without fossil fuel consumption) from wind, light, water flow, and new advanced technologies using key wavelengths of vibration to directly access unlimited etheric reservoirs of power, including the Earth's magnetic fields.

Having a steady and unlimited source of electrical power, independent of fossil fuel consumption, enables a different approach to vehicle use. A selection of various electric powered vehicles would provide for around 95% of transport needs in and around the community for both people and goods of all kinds, provided that battery recharging facilities were sufficient. Locally produced vegetable oil would be available to power diesel engines on journeys further afield. Multiple techniques for producing unlimited supplies of electricity will be further explored and developed.

Using deep understandings of Nature's vast resources, natural materials would be substituted for synthetic manufactured products—for example, using natural readily available fibres to make rope. New foods would be introduced in palatable form to more fully utilise the broad spectrum of nutrients available from local environments.

A health and healing centre would play an important role in maintaining a fully functioning community through addressing physical, emotional, and Spiritual aspects of individuals, as well as the integration and balancing of their various layers. New technologies would be developed to provide healing energy fields as well as beneficial sound and light vibrations to enable life and healthy living to reach new heights.

A foundation understanding of the centre would be "there are no incurable diseases, only incurable people". There would be an implicit understanding that the harmonising vibration of perfectly aligned energy can overwrite any physical or emotional malfunction and restore it to harmonious and normal functioning, provided the recipient has requested the healing and is open to receiving it. Yet there will be an equal recognition that the mystery of healing is not always revealed in the cure of a physical condition.

An important and related activity would be in Spiritual education and training for members of the community and also those living in other locations. Courses and workshops would cover such subject areas as:

- *The maintenance of harmony and grounding;*
- *Spiritual healing;*
- *Nutrition;*
- *Biodynamic farming;*
- *The husbandry of animals, poultry and fish;*
- *Attuning to Fifth Dimensional Consciousness.*

This new Consciousness can be used to develop viable communities throughout the world, tuned in to the changes being embraced by the Earth as she evolves in the years up to 2012. The dissemination of this stream of information and understanding is expected to be an ongoing priority for community endeavours.

Planning a Community

The first phase involves finding a suitable location and available land in which to manifest a Fifth Dimensional Consciousness community. This would be used to create a Centre of Light to facilitate the run-up to 2012 for the beneficial evolution of those directly involved, as well as all those people who are touched by some form of outreach or direct contact. Restoring Nature to her higher rhythms and then facilitating her higher evolution is also a major objective.

The land must be relatively unpolluted in terms of agricultural chemicals, artificial fertilisers, mining, airborne contamination, as well as various forms of astral contamination derived from negative emotions and/or a dark history of war or other violence. Given the appropriate pre-conditions, the conversion to biodynamic cultivation would be faster than from conventionally farmed arable land.

Following Rudolph Steiner's inspiration, the biodynamic approach goes beyond organic cultivation because of a high degree of alignment between the gardener and the natural rhythms of the Earth and Cosmos. Planting, watering, transplanting and harvesting for each crop species is closely linked to the cycles of the Moon. Steiner's insights into the workings of Nature have created a new framework of understanding the relationship between mankind and the formative forces of Creation.

By the use of specially prepared biodynamic preparations, used in homeopathic-like dilutions, land can be reinvigorated with a restored life-force. By re-establishing our connections to the highest rhythms of the seasons, moon cycles, and the magnetic forces of the Earth, foods of the highest nutritional quality can be produced.

A vibrant landscape produces vibrant people and this Higher frequency provides insulation from the imbalance and dis-ease of the modern world. Working in harmony with Nature not only grows healthy food, but also enables much healthier people. Our future depends on being able to consistently obtain living foods as well as having the ability to live with the natural timing rhythms of the Earth. A community would aim to lead the way with hands-on demonstration and practice of these principles and understandings.

The approach is not dissimilar from the old knowledge of country people about how plant, vegetable and fruit cultivation is directly related to their environment of insects, animals, birds and "wild" Nature. The whole biodynamic system pulls together what might have been the collective knowledge of many villagers (had they ever pooled what they knew) and makes it available as a coherent body of understanding. Our aim is to demonstrate in the most practical way, the feasibility of self-sufficiency in food supply through using a deeper understanding of essential relationships inherent in the plant and animal kingdoms. Attunement on this level leads to careful preparations, instead of elaborate equipment and/or chemicals.

The chosen location would need to be an area Spiritually-designated as safe from sea or ocean inundation, coupled with a vibrational environment conducive to creative endeavour, to inspired innovation and application, as well as to Spiritual Attunement.

The facilities would include living space, meeting areas, as well as working areas for biodynamic farming development, building renovation, conversion, and construction, along with ample space for technology development. Ideally, the land surrounding the main buildings would comprise a mixture of woodland, hillside, orchard, grazing for goats and cow, a chicken–run, vegetable cultivation, meditation garden, recreational paths and a stream or river linked to a fish pond and reservoir.

Running through all aspects of the community as now conceived is the Spiritual inspiration and support giving birth to endeavour and achievement, which might have in earlier times have required a whole generation, but with inner Spiritual support might actually be manifested in a modest few months or years. It is also the Spiritual inspiration and Attunement which will attract the individual participants from many world locations. Co-creation will bring the undertaking to fulfilment.

Hopefully, many of the participants will have multiple skills within the wide range of capabilities required: biodynamic farming, food preparation, healing, building design and construction, education and communication, sacred dance and music, website and related computer skills, invention, installation and integration of alternative energy systems, as well as development of other new technologies.

A powerful healing centre would be developed, which would include current alternative approaches such as: nutrition, homeopathy, massage, acupuncture, Bowen technique, Reiki, dance movement, yoga and Chi Gung. Less well-known approaches such as Spiritual energy transmission, sound vibration, special electrical and magnetic energy fields, would play a strong role particularly in addressing seemingly "incurable" conditions.

The centre would enable all members of the community to maintain a high standard of physical health while experiencing emotional warmth and stability together with Spiritual harmony and opening, not withstanding any mass difficulty or epidemics which might be prevalent in the outside world. A significant part of the centre's work would be for visitors requesting treatment, either in person or at a distance. Educational and training programmes would be created to enable other communities and alternative health centres to provide similar treatments in their own locations.

An important part of self sufficiency is finding new sources to provide power for heating, lighting, cooking, transportation, construction and computing. It appears quite probable that availability of petroleum products and natural gas will become unreliable as well as overly expensive as time goes on, particularly if any more oil and gas fields worldwide are adversely affected by future earthquakes, hurricanes and coastal storms. Centrally generated electricity has become partially dependent on natural gas and hence vulnerable to ever diminishing supply.

There are several interim sources of power to generate electricity for use in all the applications mentioned above: using wind propellers, solar panels, and running water–driven generators. A combination of all three approaches can provide a regular power supply in most weather conditions. Battery back-up would bridge most gaps in electricity generation, like on a still freezing night.

But these sources are regarded as stepping stones while advanced technologies based on etheric enhancement are developed for regular usage. Prototypes already exist for electric motor/generator combinations, which produce significantly more current than they consume and can produce a more healthy type of electricity. The vibrational frequency of such electricity so generated sets up an energy field conducive to the flourishing of human bodies; that is a field of negative ions producing feelings of heightened physical and emotional wellbeing. The development challenge is of an engineering nature rather than exploring a new concept.

Conversions of reciprocating engines to run safely on vegetable oil or water are also advancing. These would be very helpful in extending the life of cars and trucks which currently run on petroleum products. The alternative-fuelled engines would also be valuable for use as powerful back-up generators.

A different application of new technologies is for devices using light and sound to promote healing and well being for the humans within range. Computer-based analysis of multiple measurements of energy flow (or the lack of it) in a body's meridians can provide accurate diagnosis and insights into the functioning of individual organs, glands, nerves, joints, as well as brain function, immune system and inner communication systems. The systems then prescribe treatments within nutritional, homeopathic, flower remedy, and radionic spheres of understanding.

The artistic, creative and other Spiritual activities which feed the Human Soul are important parts of community life. Sacred dance, music, visual arts, interior design, contribute directly to the health and well being of the community, while being fully worthwhile in their own right.

Colour and sound vibration, sacred dimensions, and special wavelengths are the building blocks for creating conditions that spawn the joyful experience of higher awareness. These attractive energies will support all who are drawn to this community and when combined with specific programmes of training and orientation will allow the unified growth of the community.

The essence of the plan for the new community is to find new ways of organising and undertaking the business of human living on Earth; ways which have the most positive impact on the land, the air, all aspects of Nature within the environment, and the people who live within it. Sustainable power generation and food production, buildings and land use, which promote both human vitality and health of Nature's realms, are important aspects of what we plan to create--a twenty first century revolution of human life on Earth. Attunement at all levels from the most mundane and earthbound to the most subtle and ethereal will be the basis of the work to be done.

The Spiritual Management Framework

It is our clear intention that the communities be founded on Heart-Consciousness and Love-based actions. In this light, finding the silence within, which is the true wellspring of Love, will be at the core of our work. Dedicated Attunement to Spirit is the source of understanding which provides a natural alignment for and within groups working together. The Findhorn concept of focalisation uses these understandings and thus provides a consistent approach to sound decision-making compatible with an overall Divine Plan of community evolution.

These approaches can sound quite Utopian when faced with such hard decisions like choosing priorities for the allocation of resources. However, once practised, they provide a strong structure for operating the whole organisation within Divine Attunement. The recognition that there exists a detailed and intricate Spiritual Plan for the community and its highest evolution to Fifth Dimensional Consciousness, provides a clear approach to finding the way through many situations and challenges without precedent in our lifetimes or those of our ancestors.

Depending always on the size of the initial investment, the goal is to develop a high level of self sufficiency, building up to reach a 95% level after two years or so. The anticipated 5% of needs at that time needing to be obtained from outside the community would be financed by the sale of goods and services to on-site visitors and to other communities. Some of the initial investment would be used for medium-term secure storage of industrial supplies and spare parts (for engines, motors, electrical components, etc.) and of household supplies like dental care items, nutritional supplements, natural cleansers, and clothing.

As new technologies, materials, skills, and crafts are developed, it is expected that replacement products can be substituted in some or most of the above categories. What is not known yet is which items can be locally produced using the resources available at particular points in time.

Attunement and Fifth Dimensional Consciousness

At the core of the Community's process of creation would be a meditative group who meet weekly to attune and project concentrated love energy to all parts of the community's functions and operations. This practice is based on the achievements of Spiritual healing and Creation groups in different parts of the world. By connecting through an Illuminated Web of connection to Light Beings on other planets, solar systems and galaxies, an infinite supply of Illumined Love energy is made available to heal and to renovate individuals, places, and situations.

We have found, and continue to find that major change and movement happens for the highest evolutionary interests of whoever and whatever has been requested. This Transformative power is being made available for the creation, development, and protection of the Community in all its aspects. Financial resources, people with extraordinary skills, land and buildings, inspirational designs and technology are all facilitated in their coming forward by the various Spiritual energies dedicated to helping the Earth's evolution. As the energies of attraction pull in the resources of all kinds necessary for the creation of the Community, a related energy of concentrated love acts as a cordon or boundary to insulate from any less than positive or actually discordant energies outside.

We feel that we are still at the early stages of interacting with this Fifth Dimensional source of Light, Love, inspiration and protection. It seems that regular Attunement with this frequency enables the participants to continually expand their consciousness, so facilitating the use of wave communication instead of words. This enormous expansion of "bandwidth" opens the doors to vast new worlds of understanding, development and practice.

According to the American Indian wisdom, we are entering a time of great purification as we make the transition to Fifth Dimensional Consciousness. Concomitant with major physical changes on Earth, there will be those who seek to live in harmony with the rest of Creation. Sensitive co-existence with other life is recognition of the true extent of family. The Fifth Dimensional society is shaped by the feminine paths of cooperation, unity, inclusiveness, non-competitiveness, service rather than dominance, use of psychic and Spiritual gifts, and living in conscious harmony with Nature's ways. This would facilitate a renewed society of women and men as equals

During this transition, each of us is being called to serve the Great Spirit, that Centre of Consciousness from which everything derives its Being. This level of Attunement to Spirit will facilitate bringing harmony into all human endeavours, to bring an end to the pollution of Earth, as well as support plant and animal species. We would once again become caretakers of Earth's ecosystems. And as the Cosmic vibration becomes more and more refined, these Fifth-Dimensional qualities and practices become wholly attainable.

An Invitation

This proposal will be developed in depth as more relevant insights and connections emerge. It will be circulated to interested individuals to stimulate involvement and feedback, as well as attracting funding contributions.

You are invited to contact the author if any part of this proposal arouses your interest, or you feel an attraction to being involved with a project such as this Community. It is intended to initiate planning groups as an initial step in preparing for 2012. As each group progresses, there would be plenty of scope for different kinds of involvement: becoming a departmental specialist, a communication/liaison person, a searcher for a suitable physical location, or as an outside supporter and participant, with an option to become more deeply involved as the project evolves.

Contact information

Andrew Smith at:

selfsufficientcommunities@yahoo.co.uk

Or mail to;

Pengerd Cottage, West Pennard,
Glastonbury, Somerset, BA6 8NH